T0290543

Rebranding

AMERICAN ASSOCIATION *for* STATE *and* LOCAL HISTORY
BOOK SERIES

Series Editor

Rebecca K. Shrum, Indiana University-Purdue University Indianapolis

Managing Editor

Aja Bain, AASLH

Editorial Board

ABOUT THE SERIES

The American Association for State and Local History Book Series addresses issues critical to the field of state and local history through interpretive, intellectual, scholarly, and educational texts. To submit a proposal or manuscript to the series, please request proposal guidelines from AASLH headquarters: AASLH Editorial Board, 2021 21st Ave. South, Suite 320, Nashville, Tennessee 37212. Telephone: (615) 320-3203. Website: www.aaslh.org.

ABOUT THE ORGANIZATION

The American Association for State and Local History (AASLH) is a national history membership association headquartered in Nashville, Tennessee, that provides leadership and support for its members who preserve and interpret state and local history in order to make the past more meaningful to all people. AASLH members are leaders in preserving, researching, and interpreting traces of the American past to connect the people, thoughts, and events of yesterday with the creative memories and abiding concerns of people, communities, and our nation today. In addition to sponsorship of this book series, AASLH publishes *History News* magazine, a newsletter, technical leaflets and reports, and other materials; confers prizes and awards in recognition of outstanding achievement in the field; supports a broad education program and other activities designed to help members work more effectively; and advocates on behalf of the discipline of history. To join AASLH, go to www.aaslh.org or contact Membership Services, AASLH, 2021 21st Ave. South, Suite 320, Nashville, TN 37212.

Rebranding

A Guide for Historic Houses, Museums, Sites, and Organizations

Jane Mitchell Eliasof

ROWMAN & LITTLEFIELD
Lanham • Boulder • New York • London

Published by Rowman & Littlefield
An imprint of The Rowman & Littlefield Publishing Group, Inc.
4501 Forbes Boulevard, Suite 200, Lanham, Maryland 20706
www.rowman.com

86-90 Paul Street, London EC2A 4NE

British Library Cataloguing in Publication Information Available

Library of Congress Cataloging-in-Publication Data

Names: Eliasof, Jane Mitchell, 1961- author.
Title: Rebranding : a guide for historic houses, museums, sites, and
  organizations / Jane Mitchell Eliasof.
Description: Lanham : Rowman & Littlefield, [2022] | Series: American
  Association for State and Local History book series | Includes
  bibliographical references and index.
Identifiers: LCCN 2021037550 (print) | LCCN 2021037551 (ebook) | ISBN
  9781538148891 (cloth) | ISBN 9781538148907 (paperback) | ISBN
  9781538148914 (epub)
Subjects: LCSH: Historical museums—Public relations. | History—Societies,
  etc.—Public relations. | Historical museums—Marketing. | Branding
  (Marketing)
Classification: LCC AM124 .E45 2022 (print) | LCC AM124 (ebook) | DDC
  659.2/906—dc23
LC record available at https://lccn.loc.gov/2021037550
LC ebook record available at https://lccn.loc.gov/2021037551

To my father and first editor, Craig Mitchell,
and his ubiquitous red pen

To Steve, Alex, and Joanna, my ever-supportive,
ever-loving home team

Contents

Preface

Picture a can of Coke, a Target bag, the Nike "swoosh," the Apple logo.

A "brand," according to the American Marketing Association, is "a name, term, design, symbol or any other feature" that identifies a product, service, or organization from others.[1] Before a new product or company hits the market, marketing experts may spend months and thousands of dollars researching, testing, and designing a brand identity. A good logo, one with "brand equity," can last for decades.

A "rebrand" gives an already established brand a new identity. Sometimes, particularly with well-established brands that consumers are emotionally connected to, rebranding can fail miserably. The Gap pulled back a new logo just six days after its launch.[2] Usually, it works. The Starbucks logo hasn't included the company name since 2011,[3] but it's so ubiquitous and well-known, you probably didn't even notice.

But the Starbucks brand is more than a logo. It's the experience you have when you enter the store, wait for the barista to put a latte on the counter, and take your first sip. If you've gone to a Starbucks once and were magically transported to one somewhere else, you'd know you were in a Starbucks even if you didn't see any brand name or logo. The Starbucks brand is as much about the experience as it is about the logo.

Chances are good you inherited your organization's "brand"—name, logo, and even the experience—from your predecessors. Maybe you've made some changes to the organization since you've come on board. Do your name and logo still reflect your organization and your audience's experiences with it? Do they appropriately convey your "brand"?

You may be wondering if it's time for a refreshed look, a tagline, or even a new name, perhaps something more in sync with who and what your organization is today. A rebrand of a historic site, museum, or organization may increase its visibility in the community, attract new audiences, and even change the trajectory of the organization's future.

As you move through the process of researching, testing, designing, and launching, the extent of your need to rebrand will crystallize. You may find your name still works, but your logo looks antiquated, doesn't work well in a digital format, or is often confused with another organization. On the other hand, you may find your name doesn't adequately represent your visitors' experiences or your organization anymore. It may prevent new audiences from finding your organization and may even be turning people away.

Rebranding: A Guide for Historic Houses, Museums, Sites, and Organizations was written to help history organizations of all sizes decide if it's time to rebrand and, if so, how to go about it. It's a step-by-step guide for executive directors, board members, leadership teams, and staff responsible for marketing, public relations, and communications. If you decide it's time for your organization to rebrand, consider sharing *Rebranding* with anyone who may be tangentially involved. The smaller the organization, the more likely a major rebranding will be "all hands on deck." Giving everyone the big picture can only help.

Other books have been written on rebranding. *Rebranding* is different in that it is focused on history sites, museums, and organizations. That's the ironic twist. We are, after all, in the business of preserving history. By changing your organization's name or logo, will you be accused of disregarding your institutional history or the legacy of your organization's founders? Will a rebrand disenfranchise your longtime (and perhaps most generous) donors? Will you be losing the brand equity you have built over the years? In *Rebranding*, you'll see how organizations preserved that history while looking to the future.

Furthermore, leaders in history organizations tend to have public history or museum studies backgrounds. Most likely, neither their experiences nor their studies have included focus groups, customer response surveys, product launches, and logo design. *Rebranding* is written for the museum professional who goes into a rebranding with basic on-the-job training in marketing and communications.

The idea for *Rebranding* grew out of my own experience as the executive director of a small historic site that was considering a change from the Montclair Historical Society to the Montclair History Center. I attended a workshop on rebranding at the American Association of State and Local History in 2014, but the three organizations that presented had rebranding budgets that dwarfed my organization's annual operating budget. Because I had spent years in marketing in a different industry before making the move to the Montclair History Center, I understood their experiences were valuable. More important, I knew they were scalable.

Before I began to write *Rebranding*, I interviewed twelve colleagues who are part of history organizations that have undertaken both a name and logo change. They represent local historical societies, historic sites, history museums, and large state organizations from Maine to Portland, Montana to Texas. Their budgets, staff size, visitation, membership, age, and endowments (if any) vary greatly. One is a new museum that changed its name before it even opened. Another "refreshed" a ten-year-old logo and name. Despite this variety, each organization loosely followed the same process and grappled with many of the same issues. Each organization deems its efforts successful.

Of note, the interviews were all conducted between April and August 2020, when the nation was in the throes of the COVID-19 pandemic. Several of the leaders had to modify their launches because of restrictions. Their creativity in shifting to virtual formats and expanding digital content is impressive.

In *Rebranding*, we'll walk through the rebranding process so you can benefit from your colleagues' experiences each step of the way, whether you are going all in with a new name or just updating your logo. After each chapter, you'll find questions that emanate from your colleagues' experiences. You can use these questions to help guide your rebranding efforts.

In Chapter 1, you will get a brief overview of the thirteen organizations that will be profiled throughout *Rebranding*. You'll "meet" your colleagues and learn about their organizations' challenges and goals. You will also find information on staff size, visitation, and operating budget.

Chapter 2 delves into why the leaders of the thirteen organizations believed it was time for change. For some, the rationale was simply a change in programming. For others, it represented a major shift in the stories they were telling or the way they were operating. This chapter encourages you to do some deep soul-searching. What is your vision and mission? Has it changed in recent years? Whom do you cater to now, and whom do you want to cater to in the future? What types of programming do you offer? Has that changed? Does it reflect the demographic of your community?

If a new name is under consideration, has your organization changed enough—or is in the process of changing—to be "worthy" of a new name? If it has not fundamentally evolved, a new name or look may appear akin to putting lipstick on a pig. As one colleague said, "If the guest's experience is not reflective of your new brand, you haven't changed a thing except for a few fonts."[4]

In chapter 3, you will learn how your colleagues collected qualitative and quantitative data (if they did) to help them decide if and how they should change. This chapter shares their experiences and includes sample documents and/or questions, cost-effective ways to run focus groups, interviews, surveys, and other ways to reach out to your audience. It will explore the importance of getting key stakeholders (e.g., board, major donors, members, community) involved in the decision-making process. It will also encourage readers to analyze the legacy of the old name or logo and whether it may be hindering advancement in certain populations.

Chapter 4 explores some of the legal options you have if you change the name. It will include information on how the thirteen organizations in the book went about it, if they would have changed anything and why.

Chapter 5 is all about selecting a new name, designing a new logo, and developing a tagline if desired. Several graphic designers and marketing organizations provide their advice on creating memorable and relevant logos. You'll also see before-and-after images from the organizations, along with the thought process behind the new designs.

In chapter 6, you will read about how the thirteen organizations orchestrated their launches, including announcements to members, website changes, social media, traditional media, brochures, signage, business systems, etc. Should the launch happen at once? Roll out over a period of weeks? The leaders interviewed for this book share their thoughts on scope and timing as well as their missteps. You'll also see how the new branding plays out across a variety of media and uses. After reading this chapter, you will be able to develop your own, personalized launch plan and timeline.

One of your biggest questions may be cost, which can vary widely throughout the country. With advice and learnings from your colleagues, chapter 7 helps you create a realistic budget tailored to your organization. It will also share information on funding sources that the thirteen organizations used to support the rebranding efforts.

Inevitably, there will be people who are not in favor of the change. The Montclair History Center had one member who angrily demanded we refund his membership fee and take him off all future mailings. Chapter 8 presents real-life examples of naysayers from the interviews with suggestions on how to respond to them. On the flip side, you'll hear some of the positive feedback that came after the thirteen organizations rebranded.

Finally, in chapter 9, you'll read about how your colleagues evaluated their organizations' successes. Interesting, none of the organizations' leaders conducted or planned to conduct formal qualitative or quantitative evaluations. In this chapter, they talk about how they measure success and share their success stories. They also give their final words of advice to people in history organizations who are starting a rebranding effort.

As you will discover as you read *Rebranding*, the location, age, and size of the organization are irrelevant. Any history organization can embark on a rebranding initiative.

NOTES

1. "Branding," American Marketing Association, accessed July 1, 2020, https://www.ama.org/topics/branding/.

2. Thomas Goeghegan, "Lessons to Be Learnt from the Gap Logo Debacle," BBC News, October 12, 2010, https://www.bbc.com/news/magazine-11517129.

3. "Starbucks Logo: A Brief Logo History and What Makes It So Great!" Logogenie, March 31, 2020, https://www.logogenie.net/blog/starbucks-logo-a-brief-history-of-their-logo-design-evolution-and-what-makes-it-so-great.

4. Judy Zulfiqar (chief strategist, Watermark Associates) in discussion with the author, August 2020.

CHAPTER 1

Thirteen Organizations That Have Rebranded

Rebranding is like a volcanic eruption. A lot of rumbling goes on beneath the surface before it spectacularly erupts for everyone to see.

For some organizations in this book, that eruption had been building up over time. For others, it happened almost spontaneously. The organizations' leaders all believed that a new look or new name was a better reflection of their organization and would help shed an old image, appear more up-to-date, or attract new audiences. Many had made fundamental changes to their organization and wanted to convey those changes to the world. Many had been considering a rebranding for years before they finally took the plunge. One museum even changed its name but held on to many elements of its former logo before it opened its doors.

That's often where the similarities ended. Some organizations are small historical societies with annual budgets of less than $200,000 and one or two staff members; others are large museums with annual budgets in the millions and comfortable endowments. Some are private, not-for-profit organizations; others are state-run and -funded. Some are located in small towns; others are in major metropolitan areas.

In this chapter, you'll "meet" each of these organizations and leaders. As the book unfolds, you'll see how each organization met the challenge of rebranding in a way that matched its budget, staff, and constituents.

AMES HISTORY MUSEUM

Ames, Iowa
www.ameshistory.org

In 1980, local historian Farwell T. Brown founded the Ames Heritage Association.[1] One of the founding members' first accomplishments was saving

Hoggatt School, Ames's first school. Since then, the 501(c)(3) nonprofit organization has become the repository for local history in Iowa State University's hometown.[2] In time, they acquired another small office building that today houses one gallery plus a few small exhibits near the entrance. In 2005, the Ames Heritage Association became the Ames Historical Society.

According to Executive Director Casie Vance, "a majority of our members are retirees" who flock to the college town in part because of the cultural activities. Because Iowa State has its own museums and archives, Casie says they try not to replicate each other, particularly with regard to collections. "If one of us gets something that makes more sense for the other institution, we pass it along."

In recent years the organization had also begun to offer more family programs to expand its audience. By 2018, the board had agreed to embark on a capital campaign to expand the space as well. Their goal was to renovate the former office building and create additional exhibit space that gave visitors a more "museum" experience.

Before kicking off the campaign, progressive board members felt it was time for the name and logo to align with these changes. "There had been a sign on the building that said Ames History Center, but we used Ames Historical Society for all advertising, programs, and events. We talked about keeping Ames History Center, but decided Ames History Museum was a better fit."[3] The Ames Historical Society officially changed its name to the Ames History Museum in 2019.

Once it was agreed upon, rebranding was swift. The board gave Casie the go-ahead in April, and by August the new name and look went live.

Today, three full-time staff members maintain the Ames History Museum, the Hoggatt School, and an extensive on-site and digital archive on an average budget of about $175,000 generated primarily through membership, donations, programs, and grants.[4] They offer programs, rotating exhibits, self-guided adult tours, and field trips for about 7,000 visitors annually.

FIRST AMERICANS MUSEUM

Oklahoma City, Oklahoma
www.famok.org

A new 175,000-square-foot state-of-the-art museum sits on forty acres in Oklahoma City, Oklahoma, within a larger 300 acres that will be developed at a later date. This museum, dedicated to telling the stories of the tribal nations in Oklahoma today, had been in the making since the 1990s. The development of the museum has endured twists and turns as the country has gone through recessions, September 11, and wars. Even the grand opening, planned for spring 2021, was pushed back with the onset of COVID-19.[5]

The idea for this museum was originally conceived in the mid-1980s when the state began looking for ways to diversify its economic platform after a downturn in the oil industry. A Price-Waterhouse study found that tourism is the state's third largest industry. Explains Shoshana Wasserman, deputy director: "Oklahoma is known for western heritage, American Indian heritage, and of course, Route 66." The state chose Oklahoma City as the site of the proposed museum because it is centrally located, has a large airport, and has a thriving tourism sector.

Although many of the tribal nations have their own smaller museums, this museum shares the collective histories of all thirty-nine tribal nations in Oklahoma. Some have been there thousands of years; others were removed from ancestral homelands across the United States and relocated to Oklahoma in the nineteenth century.[6]

The rich history, values, and cultures of the first Americans are integral to the museum's architecture and ethos. A large mound pays homage to the great mound builders and their importance to American history. The Hall of the People is supported by ten columns, representing the ten miles walked each day during the time of removal. Even the staff's email signatures identify the tribal nation to which they belong.

During the planning years, the museum was known as the American Indian Cultural Center and Museum. "It was a mouthful," says Shoshana. In December 2019, months before it was scheduled to open, the museum launched a new, less wordy, and more accurate name—First Americans Museum—with a new logo and tagline "One Place, Many Nations." "We love the acronym 'FAM' because it gave us a way to be playful and inclusive," explains Shoshana. "In our programming, educational materials, and the first-person narrative you see throughout the museum, we are trying to counteract the stoic images of Native People that have been perpetuated by others. We wanted to get that sense of play in there."

Because FAM had not opened when *Rebranding* was in development, average operating budget figures, staff size, and visitorship information were not available.

FIVE OAKS MUSEUM

Portland, Oregon
www.fiveoaksmuseum.org

Five Oaks Museum has gone through more than just a rebrand in the last two years. It's gone through a rebirth.

The changes to the organization, formerly known as the Washington County Museum, have been both systemic and seismic. Two new co-directors who already worked for the museum replaced one director. They reduced the pay differential between the highest- and lowest-paid staff.[7] They created and embraced a set of values that revolve around body, land, truth, justice, and community.[8]

The museum has transformed from one that primarily told the story of Euro-American settlers to one that shares the history, arts, and culture from the diverse people who live—or have lived—in Northwest Oregon. They have replaced one curator position with guest curators. Explains Molly Alloy, co-director: "All of our major exhibitions are led and authored by guest curators who are embedded and have meaningful cultural ties to the content that they are telling."

Their new name reflects the layered approach they are taking with history. It's named after five oak trees, located about two-and-a-half miles from their museum. Says Molly, "These five oak trees date back 500 or 600 years. They had been a place of return for native people. They were a trading site. They became a prominent site with colonial people holding governmental actions there. They have survived farming, the industrial revolution, and everything else. There's so much layered storytelling about that site, we wanted to use it as inspiration and a metaphor for how we position ourselves."

Their new name and branding went live on January 1, 2020, after about eight months of planning, with the launch of a new website, a press release, and a series of exclusive articles run in local media. They have a staff of five employees, plus guest curators and volunteers, and an operating budget of about $480,000, a little under half of which comes from the county. Five Oaks Museum does not have an endowment.

HISTORYMIAMI MUSEUM

Miami, Florida
www.historymiami.org

In 2010, the Historical Museum of Southern Florida, located in the heart of Miami, had a contract in place with a firm in Boston to lead them through a rebranding initiative. Believing their old name was antiquated and un-wieldy, the leadership team's goal was to unveil their new name—History-Miami—and logo at a seventieth anniversary event.[9]

Founded in 1940 as the Historical Association of Southern Florida, the organization opened its first brick-and-mortar museum in 1962.[10] Today, HistoryMiami Museum consists of two adjacent buildings totaling about 75,000 square feet connected by a tiled plaza. The buildings house a series of permanent and rotating exhibits that "tell Miami's stories," plus an education center and the Southern Florida Folklife Gallery, which is dedicated to documenting, presenting, and supporting the region's traditional arts and culture. Since its rebranding, HistoryMiami has diversified its audience through exhibits such as Queer Miami: A History of LGBTQ Communities; Avenues of Expression: Street Traditions in Miami; and photography exhibits by local artists.[11]

After living with its new name and logo for ten years, the leadership at HistoryMiami decided it was time for a refresh and planned to unveil it at its eightieth anniversary. They also sneaked in a tweak to the organization's name, adding "museum." Because the COVID-19 pandemic made a big reveal impossible, they rolled out the refreshed logo incrementally throughout 2020.

HistoryMiami Museum, as the organization is now called, employs just under fifty people, about half of whom work part-time, and between 80,000 and 100,000 people visit annually. The museum's annual operating budget is approximately $6 million, about a third of which comes from contributions and grants from Miami-Dade County, and has a $17 million endowment.[12]

Because Executive Director Jorge Zamanillo was a museum curator in 2010 and not part of senior leadership, he was not directly involved in the first rebranding initiative. His experience being on the outside of the rebranding effort in 2010 led to his more inclusive approach to a brand refresh in 2020.

MOAB MUSEUM

Moab, Utah
www.moabmuseum.org

Founded in 1957 as the Southeastern Utah Society of Arts and Science, the Moab Museum opened in 1958 in a small, four-room house. Over the years, the museum has been known as the Museum of Moab, Dan O'Laurie Canyon Country Museum, and the Moab Museum of Natural and Cultural History. In 2020, it became the Moab Museum.[13]

The town of Moab is the northern gateway to Canyon Country in Utah, a popular destination for mountain bikers, hikers, and other tourists. Although only 5,000 residents live in town, millions of people drive through Moab every year on a two-lane highway that leads to Arches National Park to the north and Canyonlands to the south.[14]

Several years ago the leadership of the Moab Museum had grand plans that included a $60 million capital campaign and a brand new, state-of-the-art museum. A generous donor had given them $1 million in seed money to get the process started. They hired Forrest Rogers, who had led another museum through a capital campaign, as a consultant. He reached out to a team he had worked with at a previous museum, and they got to work.

Although the board of trustees decided not to proceed with the new museum, the vision morphed into a complete revamp of their existing space (approximately 3,000 square feet), with a new, fresh focus on stories rather than objects. According to Forrest, now an interim executive director, they planned to launch the name, logo, and website when the museum opened; however, the opening was delayed because of the COVID-19 pandemic. For months, the new and improved museum stood ready, but visitors couldn't visit.

Two full-time employees and several part-timers (six to eight hours a week) work at the Moab Museum, which sees approximately 7,000 visitors annually. The museum's operating budget averages around $375,000, about 60 percent of which comes from county appropriations, and there is no endowment.[16]

MONTCLAIR HISTORY CENTER

Montclair, NJ
www.montclairhistory.org

A group of early preservationists founded the Montclair Historical Society in 1965 to save a 1796 home built by local entrepreneur Israel Crane from demolition.[17] In subsequent decades, the Society added two more buildings on an adjacent lot to its collection. One, built in 1818, was donated. One, built in 1896, was purchased. The resulting campus consists of about two acres in the middle of a densely populated suburban town about seventeen miles from New York City.[18]

The Crane House has had "three lives:" the first as the Crane family home; the second as a segregated YWCA for African American women and girls; and the third as a museum. For years, however, the story of the YWCA (1920–1965) had not been told.[19]

As people moved north to Montclair during the Great Migration, the YWCA became a central place in the Black community. Although Montclair was known for being progressive and integrated, African American residents still experienced de facto segregation and discrimination. The YWCA was a haven.[20]

By 1965, the YWCA leaders knew they needed a new building. The founders of the Montclair Historical Society purchased the house for a dollar, moved it to a new location, and began to tell the Crane family story. In

2014, the Montclair Historical Society permanently reinterpreted the house to tell a more comprehensive history that included the YWCA years.

After the reinterpretation, the name "Montclair Historical Society" felt anachronistic to the board of trustees, who unanimously voted to rebrand as the Montclair History Center. Their rationale was twofold. First, they wanted to convey that it was a place to visit, not just an organization to join. Second, and perhaps even more important, they wanted to let people know that the organization had undergone a fundamental change and was committed to telling a more inclusive and diverse history of the community. The organization's new name and look went live on January 1, 2017.

The Montclair History Center, with a staff of two full-time employees and several part-time employees and an annual operating budget of approximately $250,000, sees about 7,000 visitors annually. A private nonprofit, it does not receive municipal funding, nor does it have an endowment.

NORTHWEST MONTANA HISTORY MUSEUM

Kalispell, Montana
www.nwmthistory.org

In the late 1990s the Kalispell Central School was threatened with demolition. Built in 1894, it was a school until 1969 and then part of a community college until 1989 but had remained vacant for almost a decade. Could it be turned into a museum in a city that serves as a gateway to Glacier National Park?

Executive Director Jacob Thomas recalled the story on the night the museum unveiled its rebranding in August 2019. "The town collectively held its breath, everyone wondering what was next for such an educational landmark and architectural marvel. There were many proposals, from a café to an art gallery to a business center for non-profits. . . . But the loudest, most passionate voices seemed to belong to the Northwest Montana Historical Society, who looked to revive the dream of a world-class history institution in Kalispell."[21]

The debate was contentious. On December 15, 1997, the Kalispell City Council voted five to four to save the 22,000-square-foot building and dedicate $2.5 million to its transformation to a museum. If the city council had waited two weeks to vote, the decision would have gone the other way.[22]

Over the next twenty years, the museum struggled with its identity. Although legally incorporated as the Northwest Montana Historical Society, the museum's operating name has changed from the Northwest Montana Heritage, Education, and Cultural Center to the Central School Museum to the Museum at Central School. "There was even an attempt to brand the organization as simply 'The M,'" says Jacob.[23] In August 2019, leadership announced the museum's new name and logo at a Founders' Night and Members' Open House.

Approximately 15,000 people visit annually to tour the museum, for events, or for event rentals. The museum relies heavily on volunteers to run "front of house," says Jacob, who is the only full-time employee. The museum's other three employees are part-time. Although the town still owns the property, the museum is responsible for its operations and upkeep on an annual operating budget of $144,000. There is no endowment.

OHIO HISTORY CONNECTION

Columbus, Ohio
www.ohiohistory.org

Formerly the Ohio Historical Society, the Ohio History Connection began as a collecting institution in 1885 but has evolved into an organization that its founders would likely find unrecognizable if they could visit today.

As a state partner, the Ohio History Connection is responsible for the state's historic preservation office, state archives, and local history office. It is headquartered in Columbus, where visitors experience history through a museum called the Ohio History Center and the Ohio Village, a recreated nineteenth-century town.[24]

Its reach, however, goes far beyond the city boundaries. In 2020, the organization oversaw fifty-eight historic sites in forty counties on over 5,000 acres, connecting them into one comprehensive history network visited by over 400,000 people annually.[25] The network includes museums, historic houses, archeological sites, boats, bridges, natural history sites, and canal locks.[26] Said Jamison Pack, chief marketing officer, "We believe we may be the largest historic site system in the nation and our network continues to grow."[27]

The evolution began in the mid-twentieth century. As Jamison describes it, "The state would have a historic property and say, 'Okay, Ohio Historical Society, you take care of that.'" By the time Jamison was hired in 2013, it was clear the old name didn't adequately express the many different hats the organization wore in preserving and sharing Ohio's history. Despite the continued diversification in responsibilities, the organization was still known as the Ohio Historical Society.

After research and testing, the leadership team successfully launched a rebrand in 2014. In an organization as large and as spread out as the Ohio History Connection, change can take time. Even six years after launching,

Jamison says they are still working on co-branding throughout the network sites.

Prior to COVID-19, they were operating with a staff of sixteen full-time employees and thirty to forty part-time employees.In 2020, the Ohio History Connection's total revenue was approximately $29 million, with about one-third of that coming from state appropriations. They have an endowment of approximately $9.5 million.[28]

PEJEPSCOT HISTORY CENTER

Brunswick, Maine
www.pejepscothistorical.org

Near the rocky coast of Maine, a small historical society underwent a strategic planning process that landed them with both a ten-year vision and a new name. The rebranding for the Pejepscot History Center, formerly the Pejepscot Historical Society, was unveiled in early 2020 to coincide with Maine's Bicentennial.[29]

Executive Director Larissa Vigue Picard describes the rebranding process as a "squiggly, crazy line." "If it's a creative and honest process," she believes, "it's rarely a straight line. Somebody's going to raise something you didn't anticipate."[30]

To her point, on March 24, 2020, the board of trustees had geared up to reveal the new Pejepscot History Center logo at a festive annual meeting on the campus of nearby Bowdoin College. Their plans changed when the school shut down on March 16 because of COVID-19. "For about half a day, we thought about finding another location, but quickly realized we had to cancel," recalls Larissa. The annual meeting took place on the phone, and Larissa put the logo-imprinted cocktail napkins away for another day.

Founded in 1889, the Pejepscot History Center serves three towns—Brunswick, Harpswell, and Topsham—tucked between the Androscoggin River and the Casco Bay. The organization is steward of three buildings: the Joshua L. Chamberlain Museum, which honors the memory of a Civil War hero; the Skolfield Whittier House, one-half of an Italianate duplex, which is a historic house museum and time capsule from the late nineteenth and early twentieth century; and the other half of the duplex, which houses their administrative offices and the Pejepscot Museum and Research Center.

Pejepscot History Center employs two full-time staff members, plus a part-time development manager. Approximately 5,000 to 6,000 people visit the two sites annually. Its operating budget is about $240,000, and there is no endowment.

SOCIETY FOR HISTORY AND RACIAL EQUITY

Kalamazoo, Michigan
www.sharekazoo.org

After asking herself, "Why don't we have an African American historical society in Kalamazoo?" Donna Odom started the Southwest Michigan Black Heritage Society in her living room in 2003.

When Donna moved to the Kalamazoo area from Chicago, she started attending the local historical society meetings. She noticed they rarely talked about African American history. Around the same time, she had taken a job as an educator at the Kalamazoo Valley Museum, and one of her assignments was to research a new planetarium show on the Underground Railroad. "I saw there was a rich history in the area that included the Underground Railroad, but also African American history in general," she recalls. She called some of her friends and the Southwest Michigan Black Heritage Society was born.[31]

For the first few years of its existence, the organization focused on preserving the African American history of the area. That changed in 2010 when the Kalamazoo Valley Museum hosted an exhibit on race as a social construct and invited several other organizations to partner with them.

That partnership changed the trajectory of the Southwest Michigan Black Heritage Society, which become involved not just in preserving African American history but also in promoting racial healing. By 2015, Donna recognized the name needed to change to reflect the new dual focus. The Society for History and Racial Equity did just that, plus it had the easy-to-remember and fitting acronym SHARE. Odom says, "We brought in some guys to do a logo and it was the first time I heard the word 'rebranding.'"

Unlike other organizations profiled in this book, SHARE has an office but not a historical site. They conduct most of their programs at universities, libraries, and a local hospital's education center. The organization has an operating budget of about $135,000 and employs three part-time staff—a director, an office assistant, and a programming coordinator.[32] Most of their funding comes from grants and program admissions. SHARE does not have an endowment.

SOUTHERN CALIFORNIA RAILWAY MUSEUM

Perris, California
www.socalrailway.org

In the 1950s, the Los Angeles freeway system was under construction. Fourteen teenagers and young twenty-somethings saw "their world slipping away."

As the museum's website tells the story, "Busses were replacing Red Car and Yellow Car lines. Before long, Red Cars were stacked four high at National Metal and Steel's scrap yard on Terminal Island along with rows of Yellow Cars. The last of the 'Last Runs' were playing out." On March 23, 1956, the young men met and decided to start the Orange Empire Traction Company, dedicated to preserving the rail equipment and starting a trolley museum.[33] They chose the name because it harkened back to an early Pacific Electric train ride through the inland empire of San Bernardino, Redlands, and Riverside.[34]

In June 1956, the group adopted articles of incorporation. Three members who were over twenty-one—and therefore of legal age—signed the document. Three years later, they changed the name to the Orange Empire Trolley Museum and purchased about one hundred acres of semi-desert land on an abandoned railroad right-of-way about seventy miles southeast of Los Angeles near Perris, California. As the website says, "There was no running water, no indoor plumbing, not much of anything but trolley cars and youthful enthusiasm."[35] In 1975, the Orange Empire Trolley Museum merged with the California Southern Railroad Museum and became the Orange Empire Railway Museum.

While the official name changed to Southern California Railway Museum in 2000, the organization continued to do business as the Orange Empire Railway Museum for almost twenty years. In 2019, they went live with a new logo using their official name, Southern California Railway Museum.[36]

Today, the museum has more than two hundred streetcars and railway vehicles that visitors can explore, ride on, and even take the controls as an engineer.[37] It hosts several major events each year, including "A Day with Thomas," a week-long event that draws over 30,000 each year. A month-long Polar Express event drew 38,000 people to the museum.

The museum's staff of five relies heavily on its 1,500 volunteers to accommodate over 100,000 visitors annually. Its operating budget generally exceeds $1,000,000, with an average endowment of approximately 1.3 million.[38,39]

TWO MISSISSIPPI MUSEUMS

Jackson, Mississippi
www.mdah.ms.gov/2MM

When Hurricane Katrina blew the roof off the Old Capital Museum in Jackson in 2005, the leaders had no idea a museum dedicated to telling a comprehensive history of Mississippi wouldn't reopen until 2017. When it did, it was nothing like the old museum. In fact, it was two museums.[40]

The new Museum of Mississippi History begins with the story of the indigenous people and "tells the entire sweep of our state's history from the earliest times to the present," says Katie Blount, director of the Mississippi Department of Archives and History.

The new Mississippi Civil Rights Museum, adjacent to the Museum of Mississippi History, concentrates on events that happened in Mississippi between 1945 and 1975. Says Katie, "Those events changed the nation and the world. That story needs and deserves a closer focus, and that's what we do in the Civil Rights Museum."

Today, the two museums are separate buildings under the jurisdiction of the Mississippi Department of Archives and History. Architecturally, the Museum of Mississippi History mirrors the Archives building with large marble columns, whereas the Mississippi Civil Rights Museum is more modern. "They are separated," says Cindy Gardner, museum division director, "by one inch and some caulk." The museums have one entrance, one visitor experience desk, and one gift shop.[41]

As the leadership team planned the opening in 2017, the staff of the Museum of Civil Rights had some catching up to do. The Museum of Mississippi History had more than one hundred years of collections to draw from; the Museum of Civil Rights was just starting out. The hunt for artifacts resulted in such iconic objects as the rifle that killed Medgar Evers and a chess set made of bread and saliva by an imprisoned Freedom Rider. The museum was expected to see about 180,000 people in the first year, but expectations were exceeded when over 240,000 people visited the two museums.[42]

The branding for the two separate museums has evolved since the museums opened their doors. "Originally, the museums were put together to strengthen the project in the hope it would get funded," says Katie. "But it really became the magic of the project." Today, the Mississippi Department of Archives and History has embraced what began as an internal name, "Two Mississippi Museums," and its logo reflects this unique "two-but-one" approach.

The Two Mississippi Museums' staff of eleven serve both the Museum of Mississippi History and the Civil Rights Museum. The State of Mississippi funds the museum through an annual appropriation of about $1.7 million. The Mississippi Department of Archives and History is expected to contribute $800,000 annually.[43]

VIRGINIA MUSEUM OF HISTORY AND CULTURE

Richmond, Virginia
www.virginiahistory.org

In 1831, Andrew Jackson was president, Nat Turner led a revolt against slavery, and the newly formed Virginia Historical and Philosophical Society elected Chief Justice John Marshall as its first president and former president James Madison as its first honorary member.[44]

Today its descendant, the Virginia Historical Society, a private nonprofit organization, owns and operates the Virginia Museum of History and Culture. Jamie Bosket, president and chief executive officer, attributes recent growth to a "reimagining of the organization," brought about through soul-searching and strategic planning. "The perception rooted over so many years was that the museum, with its white stone columns and big iron door, was a place for some people but not all," he explains.

The result included a new name, a new brand identity, and a new "slate of exhibits and programs" that went live in February 2018.[45]

One of the first major exhibits was "Fresh Paint: Murals Inspired by the Story of Virginia." Local and statewide artists worked with museum curators to select artifacts from the collection and then painted murals inspired by those objects. The artists worked live, in front of audiences, in a large gallery space, "symbolizing the liveliness, the contemporary way in which you can reflect on history." He notes it was also a way to introduce the brand to a new audience, which was one of the goals of the rebranding effort.

It has an operating budget of about $8 to $8.5 million, staff of "just shy of 100," an endowment of over $40 million, and a collection of over 9 million objects representing Virginia history.[46,47] In 2019, its busiest year to date, the museum hosted approximately 110,000 visitors.

ASK YOURSELF

Before moving on to the next chapter, ask yourself which organizations introduced in this chapter:

1. Resonate with you because you saw similarities to your organization?
2. Most closely match your organization's size and budget?
3. Had similar challenges to your organization?

As you continue to read, watch closely how those organizations worked through the rebranding process.

NOTES

1. "About Ames Historical Society," Ames History Museum, accessed July 27, 2020, https://ameshistory.org/content/about-ames-historical-society.

2. "About Ames Historical Society," Ames History Museum website, accessed July 27, 2020, https://ameshistory.org/content/about-ames-historical-society.

3. Casie Vance (executive director) in discussion with author, May 2020.

4. "Average Revenue from 2016–2019, Ames Historical Society," ProPublica, accessed October 15, 2020, https://www.propublica.org/search?qss=%22ames+historical+society%22.

5. Shoshana Wasserman (deputy director) in discussion with the author, July 2020.

6. "Our National Story," First Americans Museum, accessed August 8, 2020, https://famok.org/about-us/#our-national-story.

7. Molly Alloy (co-director) in discussion with the author, May 2020.

8. "About," Five Oaks Museum, accessed August 24, 2020, https://fiveoaksmuseum.org/about/.

9. Jorge Zamanillo (executive director) in discussion with the author, July 2020.

10. "About the Museum," HistoryMiami Museum, accessed August 8, 2020, https://www.historymiami.org/museum/.

11. "Exhibitions," HistoryMiami Museum, accessed August 8, 2020, https://www.historymiami.org/exhibition/.

12. "Annual Report, 2020," accessed June 13, 2021, http://www.historymiami.org/wp-content/uploads/2021/06/HistoryMiami_Annual_Report_FY2020.pdf.

13. "About the Museum," Moab Museum, accessed August 1, 2020, https://moabmuseum.org/about/.

14. Forrest Rodgers (interim executive director) in discussion with the author, July 2020.

15. "Southwest Utah Society of Arts and Sciences IRS Form 990 2018," accessed June 17, 2021, https://projects.propublica.org/nonprofits/display_990/870255102/06_2020_prefixes_82-87%2F870255102_201812_990_2020060517178900.

16. "Crane House and Historic YWCA," Montclair History Center, accessed October 24, 2020, https://www.montclairhistory.org/crane-house-and-historic-ywca-new.

17. "Mission and History," Montclair History Center, accessed October 24, 2020, https://www.montclairhistory.org/new-mission-and-goals.

18. "Crane House and Historic YWCA," Montclair History Center, accessed October 24, 2020, https://www.montclairhistory.org/crane-house-and-historic-ywca-new.

19. "Crane House and Historic YWCA," Montclair History Center, accessed October 24, 2020, https://www.montclairhistory.org/crane-house-and-historic-ywca-new.

20. Jacob Thomas, "Opening Remarks," Founders Night and Member Reception, Northwest Montana Historical Society, Kalispell, Montana, August 9, 2019.

21. Jacob Thomas (executive director) in discussion with the author, May 2020.

22. Jacob Thomas, "Opening Remarks," Founders Night and Member Reception, Northwest Montana Historical Society, Kalispell, Montana, August 9, 2019.

23. "Ohio History Center," Ohio History Connection, accessed October 15, 2020, https://www.ohiohistory.org/visit/ohio-history-center.

24. "About Us," Ohio History Connection, accessed October 15, 2020, https://www.ohiohistory.org/about-us.

25. "Visit," Ohio History Center, accessed October 3, 2020, https://www.ohiohistory.org/visit.

26. Jamison Pack (chief marketing officer) in discussion with the author, May 2020.

27. "Ohio Historical Society Audited Consolidated Financial Statement for the Year Ended June 30, 2020," accessed June 17, 2021, https://projects.propublica.org/nonprofits/display_audit/4060720201.

28. "Mission and History," Pejebscot History Center, accessed August 1, 2020, https://pejepscothistorical.org/about-us/mission.

29. Larissa Vigue Picard (executive director) in discussion with the author, May 2020.

30. "Home Page," Pejepscot History Center, accessed August 24, 2020, https://pejepscothistorical.org/.

31. Donna Odom (executive director) in discussion with the author, May 2020.

32. "Society for History and Racial Equity IRS Form 990 2018," accessed June 20, 2021, https://projects.propublica.org/nonprofits/display_990/352211484/10_2020 _prefixes_34-36%2F352211484_201912_990EZ_2020100517349668.

33. "About Us," Southern California Railway Museum, accessed August 8, 2020, https://socalrailway.org/history/.

34. "History," Southern California Railway Museum, accessed October 19, 2020, https://socalrailway.org/history/.

35. "About Us," Southern California Railway Museum, accessed August 8, 2020, https://socalrailway.org/history/.

36. Judy Zulfiqar (chief strategist, Watermark Associates) in discussion with the author, August 2020.

37. "Home," Southern California Railway Museum, accessed August 8, 2020, https://socalrailway.org/.

38. "Southern California Railway Museum," ProPublica, accessed September 23, 2020, https://projects.propublica.org/nonprofits/organizations/956102211.

39. "Southern California Railway Museum IRS Form 990 2018," accessed June 20, 2021, https://projects.propublica.org/nonprofits/organizations/ 956102211/202001849349301960/full.

40. Katie Blount (director, Mississippi Department of Archives and History) in discussion with the author, August 2020.

41. Cindy Gardner (museum division director) in discussion with the author, August 2020.

42. Roslyn Anderson, "Two Mississippi Museums Project Celebrates One Year, Exceeds Expectations," WDAM7, December 10, 2018, https://www.wdam.com/ 2018/12/11/two-mississippi-museums-project-celebrates-one-year-exceeds-expecta tions/.

43. FY 2021 Appropriation per Katie Blount (director, Mississippi Department of Archives and History) in an email, October 2020.

44. "Our History," accessed September 8, 2020, https://www.virginiahistory.org/ about-us/our-history.

45. Jamie Bosket (chief executive officer) in discussion with the author, June 2020.

46. "Our History," accessed September 8, 2020, https://www.virginiahistory.org/ about-us/our-history.

47. "Virginia Historical Society IRS Form 990 2018," accessed June 20, 2021, https://projects.propublica.org/nonprofits/display_990/540419452/08_2020_pre fixes_52-57%2F540419452_201906_990_2020082517254519.

CHAPTER 2

Why They Rebranded

"A brand is how people feel about or experience an organization," explains Judy Zulfiqar, chief strategist of Watermark Associates, the marketing firm that works with Southern California Railway Museum. "That's where people get in a quagmire. They think it's a logo, a font, a color. The reality is a brand is the overall experience. You can change your logo and it can be the most beautiful logo on Earth, but if the experience of the guest is not reflective of your brand, you haven't changed a thing."[1]

Judy and her team at Watermark Associates have led many clients through the rebranding process. She continues, "You can come up with a snazzy logo, but if you walk into your visitors' center and it has an old carpet, dark wood, and the person who greets them isn't friendly, it doesn't matter what you did with your logo. It's not going to change your brand."

For each organization in *Rebranding: A Guide for Historic Houses, Museums, Sites, and Organizations*, rebranding included a new name. Your organization's name is the most visible part of your brand. It's used in your public relations and marketing. It's emblazoned on your website, hangs on a sign in front of your building, and is on your business card. Think of how many times a day you use it in conversation. At its best, the name tells people what your organization is and what you do and even entices people to visit. At its worst, it can be a barrier to public interest and visitation.

Although everyone had different reasons to embark on a name change, three common ideas emerged among the thirteen organizations:

- Deep-rooted, fundamental changes to the organization
- A concern over the accuracy or clarity of the name

- A desire to improve public perception and ensure people better understood what the historic museum or site is all about

Most often, it was some combination of the three.

FUNDAMENTAL CHANGE

Many of the people interviewed for *Rebranding* spoke about fundamental changes and "reimagining" their organizations. While some changes were structural or organizational, most related to how they shared history or the stories they told. For each of these organizations, change ran deep.

Six years before rebranding, the Montclair History Center leadership team decided to change the permanent interpretation and programming at one of its historic sites to include the period when it was a segregated YWCA for Black women and girls. "In 1965, when the Montclair Historical Society moved the Crane House to a new location and interpreted it to tell only the story of a white founding father, the Black community was hurt," explains Elizabeth Hynes, president of the board of trustees. "They felt the rich history of the house as a YWCA was being lost," says Elizabeth.[2]

Fifty years later, that hurt was still there. In 2011, the Montclair Historical Society embarked on "the YWCA initiative," consisting of the permanent reinterpretation of the historic house; public and school programming around the YWCA, race, de facto segregation, and redlining; and a documentary based on oral histories from the women who belonged to the YWCA. The newly reinterpreted Crane House and Historic YWCA, shown in figure 2.1, opened on October 5, 2014, with 225 guests.

The goal was to gather oral histories early in the initiative to guide content development for the entire project. "We had a difficult time finding women willing to participate, because trust wasn't there," explains Elizabeth. Eventually, seven women agreed to be interviewed on camera. *A Place to Become: Montclair Through the Eyes of the Glenridge Avenue YWCA Women (1920 to 1965)*, premiered at the Montclair Film Festival in May 2014.

"Our first rebranding was the house itself," recalls Elizabeth. "We had to replace the 'Israel Crane House' sign because it was no longer accurate."

They deliberated on how to refer to the YWCA on the sign, ultimately choosing "Historic YWCA" because as Elizabeth says, "we didn't want people showing up with gym bags ready to work out." Changing the sign to "Crane House and Historic YWCA" signaled the organization was committed to telling a broader story and embracing a more inclusive history.

The first floor now reflects different historical periods and the people who lived, worked, and played there. Educators share stories about the community's development through the perspectives of the Crane family, enslaved

Figure 2.1. Over 200 guests came to Opening Day at the reinterpreted Crane House and Historic YWCA. Harry J. Mayo III/Montclair History Center.

workers, servants, the YWCA boarders, and the women and girls who took classes and socialized at the YWCA.

Programming evolved too. The Montclair History Center now hosts an annual Price of Liberty Film and Discussion series that explores issues related to race and racial equity. Other programs include speakers about early African American families in Montclair, African American genealogy, and books on race and racial equity. The organization also began to share immigrant stories, particularly the Italian immigrants, whose lives closely intersected with African American families.

"The change was deep," says Elizabeth. "The more inclusive story became part of our DNA." Within a year, the board and staff knew the name had to change. Montclair Historical Society felt antiquated, and it disenfranchised people. It didn't let the world know the institution had profoundly changed.

In 2016, the board voted to adopt a new name. Although they discussed several options, including the Montclair History Museum and Archives, they landed on the more concise Montclair History Center. "Now when we abbreviate our name as MHC," says Elizabeth, "people no longer confuse us with Montclair High School."

Two years after the change had been made, a twelve-year-old email from 2007 surfaced. In it, the then board president and executive director discussed changing the organization's name and had even suggested "Montclair History Center." The idea never moved forward perhaps because the organization was still the Montclair Historical Society at its core.

Like the Montclair History Center, Five Oaks Museum had also undergone fundamental changes. Several years ago, Five Oaks Museum (then Washington County Museum) had seen a high turnover in leadership and urgently needed change. Despite trying different tactics to increase visitation, the results were not significant nor lasting. Molly Alloy and Nathanael Andreini had both been working at the museum for a short time and agreed to become co-directors in 2019. "We saw incredible potential. There is a real need for the kind of storytelling an institution like ours is positioned to tell and there's incredibly high public trust," says Molly. "We felt we could bring some fresh new strategies."[3]

Since they became co-director, Molly says, "we have been shifting our very deepest structures" beginning with the organizational model. By creating co-directors, they "took the top off the pyramid," as Molly says, and "adjusted the pay scale to reduce the disparity between the highest and lowest paid positions, facilitating collaboration across the organization." They adopted a set of values—body, land, trust, justice, and community—that guide their actions, exhibitions, and programs.

They shifted the stories they tell and who tells them. Descendants of the Euro-American settlers had founded Washington County Museum more than sixty years ago. Today, Washington County is one of Oregon's most diverse counties, but its exhibits and programs didn't reflect that.[4] Molly and Nathaniel replaced a single curator position, where one person authored all narratives, with a guest curator program. Today, exhibits are more inclusive, and guest curators from descendant communities tell the stories.

The first exhibit with a guest curator was a reprise of an older exhibit titled, "This Kalapuyan Land." They hired Steph Littlebird Fogel, a lifelong Oregon resident, Kalapuyan, and a member of the Confederated Tribes of Grand Ronde. She worked closely with Dr. David Lewis, tribal scholar and Grand Ronde Confederation member, to eliminate inaccuracies, stereotypes, and biases in the original text.[5] Rather than reprint the boards, they marked them up, just as an editor would, as shown in figure 2.2, and titled it "This IS Kalapuyan Land." "We took the institutional voice written by people outside of the Native community and established a Native voice on

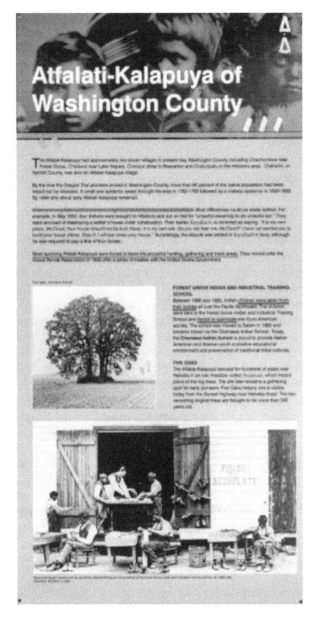

Figure 2.2. The voice of the descendant community was layered on to an exisitng exhibit at Five Oaks Museum. Five Oaks Museum.

top of it," explains Molly. "We de-colonized the museum's own exhibition to show people we will give voice away from the authority of the institution and to the descendant communities." Visitors saw the original exhibition, marked up to include the voice of the Kalapuyan people.

As part of the exhibition, Steph invited a diverse group of Native artists to display or demonstrate their art. That exhibition shaped how they build curriculum, the role of the guest curator position, and the brand itself. According to Molly, "We now consider ourselves a history, arts, and culture museum." While the changes had been happening internally, "the branding was like our 'coming out moment.'"

As the board and staff considered a new name for Washington County Museum, they wanted it to have layers, just like their exhibits. They narrowed it down to three choices:

- Washington County Museum
- Museum of the Tualatin Valley for the geographic region
- Five Oaks Museum for a nearby non-Euro-centric historic site

The staff preferred Five Oaks Museum. "There's so much layered storytelling about Five Oaks," says Molly, referring to the many peoples who used the site in its 500-year history. "We wanted to take that metaphor as an inspiration for how we position ourselves." The board agreed, and the Washington County Museum transformed into Five Oaks Museum.

Similarly, the Southwest Michigan Black Heritage Society had undergone a fundamental change. Unlike the deliberate actions taken by Five Oaks Museum, Donna Odom's organization just evolved.

Since its founding, the Southwest Michigan Black Heritage Society had concentrated on researching and documenting the area's Black history. In 2010, the Kalamazoo Valley Museum partnered with Western Michigan University to bring an exhibit on race to the museum. Sponsored by the American Anthropological Association, *Race: The Power of an Illusion*, looked at the history of race in America, identifying it as a social construct.[6]

Donna recalls, "Our organization joined that effort. We saw our role as providing the historical context." When the exhibit left the museum, her group wanted to continue offering programs that worked toward racial healing. "We brought in Tom DeWolf whose family had produced a film, 'Traces of the Trade: A Story of the Deep North,' about their ancestors' role in the slave trade."[7] He had written a companion book, *Inheriting the Trade: A Northern Family Confronts Its Legacy as the Largest Slave-Trading Dynasty in U.S. History.*

At a luncheon the organization sponsored, he introduced the film and led a discussion following the film. Through him, Donna found out about Coming to the Table, a nationwide group whose mission is "to provide leadership, resources, and a supportive environment for all who wish to acknowledge and heal wounds from racism that are rooted in the United States' history of slavery."[8] They bring descendants of both enslaved people and the people who enslaved them together for mutual healing and understanding.

"We got excited about the whole concept of racial healing," says Donna. "In 2012, we began a two-year racial healing initiative." By then, Tom De-Wolf had co-published a book, *Gather at the Table*, with Sharon Leslie Morgan, one of the descendants of the people the DeWolf family had enslaved. "They went all over the country, meeting people, going to historic sites, getting to know each other's families," says Donna. "They were living the concept of racial healing."

When the two-year initiative was over, Donna recalls, "We could see there was a real interest and hunger for the kind of programs we were doing. We were providing space for people to talk about race in a place where they could feel safe and comfortable. People always wanted more time to talk."

The board changed the organization's mission to include a dual focus of education and racial healing. The mission now reads, "to educate the community about African American heritage and foster racial healing through conversation and awareness about racism and the benefits of its elimination."[9]

Donna admits the name Southwest Michigan Black Heritage Society had been cumbersome. "Nobody could ever remember our name," she says. The new mission provided the rationale for a new name. Donna knew she also wanted a good acronym, one that was easy to remember.

The naming process was organic and simple. Donna came up with a name and brought it to her board. They liked it and the Society for History and Racial Equity—SHARE—was born.

On a much larger scale, Jamie Bosket at the Virginia Museum of History and Culture had a similar experience. "Our rebranding was so much more than a name. Our rebranding was a reimagining of the organization. We were not trying to *swap* who we are; we were trying to *grow* who we are."[10]

When Jamie joined the organization, he was impressed with the wealth of resources and depth of the collection. He recognized an opportunity to expand the audience beyond dedicated historians and history buffs to a much larger public.

The Virginia Historical Society's Board embarked on a strategic planning and visioning process and, as part of that process, began considering a new name. Says Jamie, "We knew 'Virginia' and 'history' had to be in our new name and we knew we did not want 'society.'"

They also thought about a basic regional naming structure that people were already familiar with, according to Jamie. "There's the Virginia Museum of Natural History and the Virginia Museum of Fine Arts," the latter of which is located next door. "The idea that these two core institutions are shoulder to shoulder played heavily in our minds as we went through the process." The Virginia Museum of History seemed like a natural new name.

Instead, they approved the Virginia Museum of History and Culture. "To a certain degree, 'history' and 'culture' say the same thing," reflects Jamie. "You can argue history is culture and culture is history." They chose to include both words because it provided expanded opportunities for programming. Their research also showed that younger audiences identified more with "culture." With both history and culture in the name, "we could do displays of art or innovations in science, as long as they fit within the umbrella of the Virginia story" says Jamie.

One exhibit that helped launch the reimagined museum and rebrand to the public was "Fresh Paint: Murals Inspired by the Story of Virginia." Virginia artists worked with curators to select artifacts as inspiration and then painted murals in front of a live audience. One artist chose a glass related to the Black troops that fought at the Civil War Battle of Petersburg. "As a young Black man himself, the artist painted an incredible mural of the conflict of Black soldiers stuck in the middle of this national crisis," explains Jamie. "The exhibit symbolized the contemporary way in which you can reflect on history and the marrying of fun, timely events with artifacts from the past. This is the joining of history and culture."

Across the country, Moab Museum leadership may have made the decision to rename even if they hadn't fundamentally changed by gutting their building, revamping their exhibits, and switching to an emphasis on stories rather than objects.

Over the years, the museum had several names. In 1958, the Women's Literary Society of Moab, also known as the Busy Ladies Club, received a gift of a house. They called it "The Moab Museum" and, over time, subtitled it "Canyon Country Museum." When a donor gave money to build a new museum space, they changed it to the "Dan O'Laurie Museum of Moab," then to "Museum of Moab." The board adopted yet another new name, albeit for a very short time, when they were planning the capital campaign for the new "Moab Museum of Natural and Cultural History."

Even though the board chose to renovate their existing space rather than build new, they still believed it was time for a new name. They went back into their own history and to their original name, the Moab Museum. "Since our URL was www.moabmuseum.org, it was a relatively easy case to make," recalls Forrest Rogers. "Moab Museum is simple, it's concise, it places us where we are."[11]

Forrest was also ready to replace the old logo. "It included an image based on a sculpture made for the museum. It was supposed to be a big horn sheep in the mountains, but some people thought it was kokopelli, the flute player," he says. "It was hard for people to decipher unless it was in color."

ACCURACY AND CLARITY

Southern California Railway Museum's new name didn't reflect a fundamental change in the museum's focus. It was not designed to attract new audiences or change the public's perception of who they were or what they did. The change was made to accurately place the museum in Southern California and end visitors' confusion.

The name Orange Empire Railway Museum had historical roots, but the public wasn't aware of those roots. Instead, the name just led to misunderstandings about the museum's location in Riverside County. "We were getting lots of questions because people thought the museum was in Orange County," says Judy. While Orange County is adjacent to Riverside County, the museum is more than twelve miles from its border.

When Judy's firm noticed legal documents that already said Southern California Railway Museum, "we suggested that name was more reflective of who they are and much easier for branding and marketing." The board took some time to accept the change, but the impending launch of a new website and the need to create billboards for upcoming events forced the issue. "We didn't want to create a website or put up billboards under the old name and have to change them."

The American Indian Cultural Center and Museum's team was also concerned about accuracy, but in a much different way. "Back in my mother's time," says Shoshana Wasserman, "the term was 'Indians.' It was inaccurate, but that was the term of the times. That gave way to 'Native Americans,' but as our country evolved, a large group of people born in the United States also consider themselves native to America. Then there was a shift to 'American Indians.' The Smithsonian National Museum of the American Indian and others all across the country embraced 'American Indian' saying they would give new context to the term even though it was inaccurate. And today, some of our younger people like the term 'indigenous people,' but it is very broad. No one term is ever going to fit."[12]

Shoshana draws a parallel to Europe. "We understand there are forty-four European nations with different languages and different cultural lifeways. For some reason, we have a hard time when it comes to indigenous or native peoples."

In addition to accuracy, the leadership team was concerned about memorability. The American Indian Cultural Center and Museum—shortened to AICCM—was difficult to remember both as a full name and as an acronym. "We needed a distinguishable name in the museum field, and we landed on First Americans Museum," recalls Shoshana.

"We took a bold approach," she continues. "While we were certainly not the first *citizens* of the United States (in fact, we were among the last), we were the first *peoples* of this continent. We want to own that moving forward."

The bonus was the acronym FAM. "When we looked to peer museums that have a cool vibe, they all had an acronym that's easy to manage. We love that FAM was not only short and concise, but it's inclusive," says Shoshana. "It was always our intention to be as inclusive as possible, but the process really pushed us to think in those terms and make sure we were creating a brand that everybody could feel part of. Be part of the FAMily. Join the FAM."

In a major rebranding a decade ago, HistoryMiami had been oversimplified, believes Jorge Zamanillo. "It was confusing. People were saying 'What are you? Are you a historical society? Are you a gallery?'" People thought the old museum had closed or been sold. He and the staff quietly began slipping "museum" into the name about four or five years ago. Their recent rebranding, or as Jorge says, "refresh," formally introduced "museum" into their name and logo.

There was also confusion about the spacing—more specifically, the lack of spacing. "They created this one word, "HistoryMiami," that looks really cool in print, but the people spell it wrong. To this day, they spell it wrong every time."

Another real driver behind the refresh was the logo's old bright orange color. "It was supposed to be orange red, like the Golden Gate Bridge," says Jorge. "But each printer had a different orange, so it never looked the same." Graphics were often dominated with a big block of orange and when printed on black, says Jorge, "it looked like Halloween." The organization's marketing director Michele Reese Granger says the "cinnamon" color, as she calls it, is more evocative of fall in New England than Miami.[13]

HistoryMiami kept the big "HM" in their logo, but modified it slightly, changed fonts, and adopted an aqua teal and fuchsia pink color palette. It's a color palette people know and recognize. The new design also meets all ADA accessibility guidelines.[14]

Clarity was also at the heart of Northwest Montana History Museum's name change. "If you're rolling through Kalispell on your way to Glacier National Park," says Jacob Thomas, "and you see something called the Museum at Central School, you don't know if it's a historic schoolhouse, a history museum, or some other kind of museum," as shown in figure 2.3. "We had a museum named after a school that few people even remembered."[15]

They considered several names including the Northwest Montana Heritage Center and the Museum of Northwest Montana. The Northwest Montana History Museum clearly told visitors what to expect from the museum.

Their decision to rebrand was "market-conscious," Jacob says. They wanted people—both local and visitors—to immediately understand it was a museum dedicated to preserving and presenting northwest Montana's history.

Figure 2.3. The "Public School" sign on the building confused visitors. Was it a school or a museum? Northwest Montana History Museum.

PUBLIC PERCEPTION AND UNDERSTANDING

The five leaders at the former "historical societies" interviewed for *Rebranding* (Ames, Montclair, Ohio, Pejebscot, and Virginia) said one reason they considered a name change was because of the public's perception of "historical society." Even if that wasn't their primary reason to change, they steered clear of the term as they contemplated new names.

Each person said they believe "historical society" conjured up images of an exclusive, nondiverse, membership-only organization of primarily older adults. It didn't attract, and perhaps even discouraged, visitors. This idea isn't new. In the mid-twentieth century, *New Yorker Magazine* published a cartoon showing two women sipping cocktails in a well-appointed apartment. The caption read, "I've been thinking of joining the historical society, but I don't want to be that sort of person."

When the Ohio Historical Society set out to rebrand in 2013, the organization had fundamentally changed, but it had been a gradual process over many decades. The leadership team knew "historical society" no longer accurately described all they did as the state preservation arm, their large statewide network of sites, and their own museum and village. But those changes weren't what led to rebranding.

They realized public perception was most problematic. Early focus groups demonstrated people viewed the institution as out-of-date, exclusive, and not for them. According to Jamison Pack, "They didn't say 'It's this amazing organization that has more than fifty places where I can take my family on any given weekend.'"[16] Name was clearly a barrier.

Jamison says the creative team initially presented about twenty potential names. They whittled that down internally to about five names and then agreed on Ohio History Connection.

The term *connection* echoes their former mission, which included the phrase "help people connect with Ohio's past to understand the present and create a better future." It also connotes a network of sites all united under one large umbrella organization.

The Pejepscot Historical Society's Board embarked on an extensive strategic planning effort to ensure they had a singular vision for the organization and a plan to achieve it. Part of the plan included expanding their audience and exploring the possibility of a new name and rebrand.

From the outset, there were two givens. First, the board was certain "society" should not be included in the new name. Second, "'Pejepscot' was nonnegotiable," says Larissa Vigue Picard. "Yes, it's a difficult word to pronounce, but it's a great conversation starter. It is a Wabanaki word that means 'crooked like a diving snake' or 'the long, rocky rapids of the river.' For us, it's an important place name."[17]

The board considered "Pejepscot Center for History" and "Pejepscot History Center," ultimately opting for the shorter name that sounded more inclusive and up-to-date than their former name.

The logo itself had its drawbacks, even though it had been in use for less than five years. It featured a "very distinguished, classy looking cupola" echoing one atop the Skolfield-Whitter House. Larissa admits it was iconic, "but it had nothing to do with the Chamberlain House," the organization's other property. While the logo helped identify one of their buildings, "it didn't really talk about what we did."

At the Ames Historical Society, Casie Vance says they also believed a new look and a new name would appeal to younger audiences. She recalls, "Our old logo *looked* historical." Their logo, which consisted of their name stacked in white type on a field of brown, didn't size up or down well. "We wanted something that was more useful in marketing, something that wasn't just our name."

Additionally, their upcoming capital campaign supported the development of new galleries and hands-on activities that would appeal to younger audiences and families. As they moved forward, they wanted the public to know, as Casie says, "We really are more of a museum than historical society."[18]

For the Two Mississippi Museums, the need to change public perception was more nuanced than just dropping an outdated phrase. Their need to embrace their "oneness" quickly became apparent after the two museums opened in 2017. "People would say, 'I'm going to the Black museum,'" recalls Pam Junior, director of the Two Mississippi Museums. "It was terrible, but we'd use it as a chance to educate them. 'No, there's no Black museum,' I would say. 'There's no white museum. There are Two Mississippi Museums.'" Someone even accused them of having two museums that were "separate, but equal," harking back to Jim Crow segregation.[19]

The need to address the public's misunderstanding led them back to the early days of planning. "In 2011, both of the museum efforts—the new history museum and a private civil rights museum—were stalled," remembers Katie Blount. "Two of our Board members, former governor William Winter and Judge Ruben Anderson, went to Governor Haley Barber and proposed the idea of joining these two projects, putting them both under the Department of Archives and History, and building them together in downtown Jackson, as shown in figure 2.4. Governor Barber got behind the idea and led the campaign to approve the initial bond funding of $40 million to build the museums and develop the exhibits."[20] The "two-but-one" concept was born.

Figure 2.4. The Mississippi Museum of History (left) and the Mississippi Civil Rights Museum (right) are two distinct museums, yet they make up the Two Mississippi Museums. Photo by Tom Beck. MDAH.

Katie and Cindy Gardner both recall struggling with the concept during development. They wanted each museum to have its own identity, but would the public understand how they were connected? Would they compete for fundraising dollars? Would there be competition among staff?

Six years later, the two separate museums opened, each with its own staff, fundraising campaigns, and marketing departments. Within a year, they realized that wasn't working. "We needed to join the two under strong leadership with one person who has a single vision for both museums," says Katie. Under Pam's leadership, the two museums merged and the "Two

Mississippi Museums" name, which had been used internally since 2011, became public.

Says Katie, "The power of the story, the power of the fundraising appeal, the fact that people want to be involved are all due to the decision to combine these two museums." She recalls how former governor Winter, a strong advocate for racial justice and social equality and the museums' board president, had spoken eloquently about the importance of *all* people walking into *one* building together to learn *all* of our stories. "I thought there was poetry to that concept."

VISION AND MISSION?

When asked whether the development of a new vision and mission preceded their rebranding, the leaders' answers were surprisingly inconsistent. For some organizations, a newly adopted or reaffirmed mission directed their rebranding efforts. For others, revising the mission statement came later, as if they were playing catch-up to all the changes their organizations had undertaken.

At the Virginia Museum of History and Culture, Jamie says, "By early 2017, we had our new strategic plan in place, we had reaffirmed our mission and had formalized our vision, and we were deep in the process of resolving our brand."

Similarly, at the Pejebscot History Center, rebranding was part of a much larger strategic planning process. They examined their existing mission, shortened it, and created a vision statement from it, but it stayed essentially the same. They had assumed a rebranding would occur when they began, and the strategic planning process confirmed it.

At SHARE, the decision to expand to a dual mission, change the name, and rebrand was almost simultaneous. "I knew we needed to change our mission," recalls Donna. "We were going to take on this dual mission of doing history and promoting racial healing."They welcomed the opportunity to change a name they didn't like.

The Ohio History Connection tweaked their mission from "Spark discovery of Ohio history, help people connect with Ohio's past to understand the present and create a better future" to "We spark discovery in Ohio stories" *after* the rebranding had taken place.

Five Oaks Museum had put a new vision and mission on hold and instead relied on their core values to shape their new identity. The team plans to revisit a mission and vision in the future.

The Montclair History Center's vision and mission had been approved by the board in 2012, just as the YWCA initiative was getting underway, and five years before the rebrand. By adding the words "share the stories of the people who made Montclair what it is today," the idea was to tell more inclusive stories. As part of an upcoming strategic planning process, the board will address the possibility of updating their mission statement to ensure it reflects the fundamental changes in the organization.

The common thread, regardless of whether it was articulated in a formal mission statement, was that everyone had a strong sense of their organizations' identities and plans for the future.

In this chapter, we talked about why the board and staff of the thirteen organizations believed they needed to rebrand. In chapter 3, we'll talk about some of the tools they used to vet their ideas, the importance of getting key stakeholders involved, and addressing concerns about the legacy of the old name or logo.

ASK YOURSELF

As you consider rebranding, or as Jorge says, a "refresh," ask yourself:

1. Think about your organization's identity and plans for the future:
   a. Has your vision and mission changed in recent years?
   b. Whom do you cater to now and whom do you want to cater to in the future?
   c. What types of programming and exhibits do you offer? Have they changed? Do they reflect the demographics of your community?
2. When we are familiar with a space, we often overlook the torn carpet, dark lighting, or musty smell. Think about your museum or site from the visitor's point of view.
   a. What is their experience like?
   b. Does it match your brand identity (logo, fonts, colors, type)?
3. Do you think you need a name change as part of the rebranding process? If so:
   a. Has your organization undergone fundamental changes that should be reflected in a new name? If so, can you clearly articulate them?
   b. Is your old name accurate? Does it correctly identify your location? Is the language correct (e.g., American Indian versus First American)? Do you plan to change it in the near future?
   c. Does your organization's name convey to the public who and what your organization is today? Has your single historic house become

a historic village? Has your organization expanded or changed its focus? Does the name reflect your overall brand experience?

4. Do you have a clear sense of the future of your history organization? Can you articulate it clearly and succinctly?

5. If your name is right, but you believe it's time for a logo change:
    a. Why isn't your current logo working for you?
    b. Is it difficult to use? Why?
    c. Does it look outdated?
    d. Does it accurately reflect your overall brand experience?

NOTES

1. Judy Zulfiqar (chief strategist, Watermark Associates) in discussion with the author, August 2020.

2. Elizabeth D. Hynes (president, board of trustees) in discussion with the author, October 2020.

3. Molly Alloy (co-director) in discussion with the author, May 2020.

4. "2020 Most Diverse Counties in Oregon," Niche, accessed November 1, 2020, https://www.niche.com/places-to-live/search/most-diverse-counties/s/oregon.

5. "This IS Kalapuyan Land," Five Oaks Museum, accessed November 1, 2020, https://fiveoaksmuseum.org/exhibit/this-is-kalapuyan-land/.

6. Donna Odom (executive director) in discussion with the author, May 2020.

7. "Synopsis, Traces of the Trade," accessed November 1, 2020, www.tracesofthetrade.org/synopsis/.

8. "About Us, Coming to the Table," accessed November 1, 2020, https://comingtothetable.org/about-us/.

9. "Home," Society for History and Racial Equity, accessed November 1, 2020, http://sharekazoo.org/.

10. Jamie Bosket (chief executive officer) in discussion with the author, June 2020.

11. Forrest Rogers (interim executive director) in discussion with the author, July 2020.

12. Shoshana Wasserman (deputy director) in discussion with the author, July 2020.

13. Michele Reese Granger (marketing director) in discussion with the author, January 2021.

14. Jorge Zamanillo (executive director), in discussion with the author, July 2020.

15. Jacob Thomas (executive director) in discussion with the author, May 2020.

16. Jamison Pack (chief marketing officer) in discussion with the author, May 2020.

17. Larissa Vigue Picard (executive director) in discussion with the author, May 2020.

18. Casie Vance (executive director) in discussion with the author, May 2020.

19. Pamela Junior (director, Two Mississippi Museums) in discussion with the author, August 2020.

20. Katie Blount (director, Mississippi Department of Archives and History) in discussion with the author, August 2020.

CHAPTER 3

Testing the Water

"As part of the interview process a Trustee asked me, 'Do you think our name is a barrier to our growth and success?'" says Jamie Bosket, recalling his job interview with the Virginia Historical Society. "I said, 'Yes, I think it is, but I wouldn't act on it without backing it up with research.'"[1]

You may have a gut feeling the overall brand feels outdated or the name is no longer working for you, but, like Jamie, you want to confirm your hunch through research. There are two kinds of research you can turn to—qualitative and quantitative. Qualitative research is based on ideas, thoughts, and perceptions. Focus groups, one-on-one conversations, and community gatherings are all examples of qualitative research. Quantitative research is based on numbers. Polls and surveys are simple tools for obtaining this kind of research. When money is no object, market researchers use both types of research before making final recommendations or decisions.

Your organization, like many of those in *Rebranding: A Guide for Historic Houses, Museums, Sites, and Organizations,* may not have that luxury. In fact, a couple of people said they simply asked a few colleagues or key stakeholders what they thought and then went ahead with the process. Others, particularly larger organizations, hired consulting firms to help them through the process. Most fell somewhere in the middle. They may have brought some people together to get their opinions, sent out a small survey, or talked to a few people one-on-one.

The key takeaway for this chapter is that, even if you can't afford to hire a market research consultant or firm, you can still do some research internally at a relatively low cost. Your research will help you determine whether a rebranding will help or hurt and whether it is needed or wanted. This chapter will walk you through that process and give you some tips and tools to guide you on your way.

UNDERSTAND YOUR AUDIENCES

The goal of your research is to help you understand your audiences. Begin by making a list of your past, present, and future audiences. How important are they to your organization and why? What do they think of your organization? Is your name and logo in sync with your brand and visitor experience? Do they think a rebranding is necessary? Why or why not? Will they be advocates for you?

At most organizations, the decision to rebrand begins at the board level. Several people interviewed said they wanted a unanimous vote from the board in the record before they moved forward. Similarly, at Northwest Montana History Museum, Jacob Thomas recalls, "Everybody on the Board was super supportive of changing, whether it was someone who joined a year ago or a senior advisor. A past president said, 'This name has never worked for the organization.'"[2] Casie Vance, at the Ames History Museum, says the board president and several younger board members advocated for the change and encouraged the rest of the board to be open to it. At the Montclair History Center, the board's buy-in was unanimous from the day the idea was first floated. The Pejepscot History Center Board came to the united decision to rebrand as part of a strategic planning process.

Next, consider your key stakeholders, which differ from organization to organization. At the Ohio History Connection and the Two Mississippi Museums, state legislative bodies are important audiences. First American Museum's key stakeholders include the City of Oklahoma City, tribal nations, and private citizens who have supported the mission.

At the Northwest Montana History Museum and the Southern California Railway Museum, museum founders are still active. Think about whose buy-in can be most influential and whose negativity could be most damaging to your organization.

Another audience is the people who know your organization well, including members, visitors, and donors of all sizes. They know what your organization stands for and the programs you offer and are interested in your organization's future. Consider people who used to be active but have drifted away. Is there a common thread among this audience? What reasons do they have for becoming less involved?

Other community groups—libraries, senior organizations, other museums, business districts, schools, universities, churches—can also provide valuable insight into your community, trends, and needs. Which groups do you partner with? Which would you like to engage with in the future?

The general public is "everyone else" and may represent your largest growth area. It includes people in your community who have never visited your site, future audiences, and travelers passing through your town. You may find their perceptions—if they are aware of your organization at all—

differ significantly from your other audiences. Because this audience is so vast and represents growth, consider segmenting it by age, geography, race, ethnicity, or interest.

TIMING

Before you begin your research, ask yourself what you want to know about these audiences and why it would be helpful. Knowing *who, what,* and *why* you want to know helps determine *when* to do it.

If you conduct research early in the process, you can collect baseline data about the public's perception of your existing brand. It can validate or negate the need to change. If you choose to move forward, this research gives you an objective rationale to present your case to constituents, the media, and people who think a change is unnecessary. It allows you to back up that gut feeling with research.

You may be so sure your organization needs to rebrand that you're ready to proceed without formal research. Perhaps you've already begun the rebranding process, but you want to test a few names or logos before choosing one. A few one-on-one interviews, a poll, or focus group may help you make the right choice. Finally, after you've rebranded, research could help document the success of rebranding, particularly if you received funding for it and want to include it in a final grant report.

Once you've determined your goals, audience, and timing, it's time to choose your market research tools. The remainder of this chapter describes common qualitative and quantitative research tools, many of which can be scaled up or down depending on your budget. With the increased use of web-conferencing since COVID-19, many of these tools can be reproduced online if needed, particularly if you want to reach people who are not located near your site or each other.

QUALITATIVE RESEARCH

Focus Groups

In a traditional focus group, a trained moderator meets with eight to twelve people at a focus group facility to explore a group's ideas about a topic. If, for example, you were launching a new soap, the group might weigh in on its color, fragrance, and lather. Participants receive compensation for their time, including their travel time and the sixty to ninety minutes they spend in the focus group. Usually, representatives from the sponsoring organization sit in a separate room behind a one-way mirror that allows them to observe without influencing responses. A market research firm recruits participants, conducts the focus groups, and provides the client with an analysis of the groups' responses.

In an optimal world, at least two focus groups are held using the same set of questions. Because one or two people with strong opinions and persuasive personalities can sway a group's response, multiple groups give a less biased perspective that can be extrapolated to a wider audience.

A focus group project can cost between $4,000 and $12,000,[3] a fee that can be daunting. The Ohio History Connection and the Montclair History Center, however, found ways to conduct focus groups without the high price tag.

When the Ohio History Connection began their rebranding, a local Columbus-based ad agency offered to conduct ten focus groups pro bono. "It began with a question about membership," recalls Jamison Pack. "There was an assumption people didn't know us and therefore didn't know we were a membership organization."[4]

The agency recruited "self-identified history lovers and moms" for two focus groups in five different Ohio communities to better understand their awareness and perception of "Ohio Historical Society." Through the focus groups, says Jamison, "we were able to clarify there was a strong awareness around Ohio history and the resources we manage. Perception was the issue. We saw feedback that we were an exclusive organization and not relevant."

Through their research they learned that "Ohio Historical Society" sounded outdated and elitist. "It kills the historian," she continues, "but they perceived us as 'antiquated.' They told us, 'When I think of the Ohio Historical Society, I think of an exclusive club. That's not for me.'"

Working with the ad agency, leadership shifted their discussion from membership to a larger discussion of identity. According to Jamison, the agency told them, "Your name, which is what the people in the focus groups identify with, is a barrier to them seeing you as a place for an experience." A search for a new name began.

The Montclair History Center didn't conduct focus groups during their rebranding process because of the prohibitive cost. However, about two years after their rebranding went live, a business professor at nearby Seton Hall University invited them to participate in a joint marketing project. The benefits were mutual. Their students gained experience organizing, conducting, and analyzing focus groups; the nonprofit got the benefit of a quasi-professional focus group. The only cost to the Montclair History Center was the participants' compensation—a $25 Starbucks gift card—which was welcomed by the target audience of college students and recent graduates.

Because the Montclair History Center had identified young adults as a potential for audience expansion, the fit was natural. Over the course of the semester, a team of students worked with museum staff to craft focus group questions, just as a professional agency might. At the end of the project, the students presented a final report to museum staff and select board members. It included types of programming that excited this age group, preferred length and format of tours, acceptable price points for events and programs, and preferred forms of communication.

On the day of the focus groups, representatives from the Montclair History Center watched from behind the mirror. In addition to the insights the focus groups provided about programming and marketing to this audience, the groups indirectly confirmed the value of the rebrand. "Everyone was open to coming to the Montclair History Center for programs and events," recalls Elizabeth Hynes. "There was no perception that it was 'exclusive' or 'old-fashioned,' terms that emerged on the pre-rebranding online survey from this audience demographic.[5]

Community Gatherings

Unlike focus groups, in which a random sampling of a target audience is invited, community gatherings or "charrettes" are designed to elicit information from a specific group of people. Your list may include members, former members, large donors, community organizations (e.g., the public library, the board of education, the Rotary Club), and other cultural institutions (e.g., a local art museum, nearby historical societies).

The beauty of a community gathering is the creative synergy that often develops in the room. Ideas build on other ideas. It's also a great way to educate community influencers about your organization and get them involved. The drawback is, like a focus group, a room can be easily swayed by strong personalities or someone who dominates the conversation.

Begin by identifying your goals. A community gathering can help you explore ideas for how to be more relevant to the community, understand what the community thinks of your organization, or see if the changes you have already made to your organization have been noticed. Although you may also want to share your ideas for a new name or logo, that discussion should be part of a larger dialogue about your overall brand.

Once you know what you want to accomplish, begin planning the meeting logistics.

- Determine the number of meetings you want to hold. Because community gatherings are relatively inexpensive, you may want to field more than one. Multiple meetings allow people to attend one that works best with their schedule. It also gives you the opportunity to invite members and donors to one meeting and community representatives to another.

- Choose a time that works best for your group. Lunchtime is a great time to gather community organizations. Evenings or weekends may be better for members. Aim for a length of an hour or two at most.
- Select a moderator who can facilitate a meeting skillfully, knowing when to explore an idea or concept more deeply and when to move on. A strong moderator lets the conversation unfold for a bit, but once it begins to digress from the goals too greatly, knows how to bring the focus back. Someone affiliated with your organization may be effective, but if homegrown talent is not available, consider asking someone from another organization in town or even hiring a professional.
- Choose your location. First, make sure the room can comfortably accommodate your group. Second, make sure it's convenient and has plenty of parking. Third, if you are engaging in potentially controversial topics, you may want to find neutral space away from your site.
- Invite guests. Groups of between ten and twenty people are most effective. Invite more because it's unlikely everyone you invite will attend.
- Arrange to record the meeting. If this isn't possible, assign one or two scribes to take detailed notes.
- Order food. Unlike focus groups, you usually don't need to pay participants to come to a community gathering, but participants always appreciate coffee and a light breakfast or sandwiches.
- Consider giving each attendee a "swag bag" with items from your museum shop or a book as a thank you. Before you grab a branded tote bag, remember your brand is potentially changing and you may not want to continue to disseminate the old logo. Conversely, if you have already decided on a new name or logo, it could be the perfect time to introduce it.

Next, plan your meeting. A printed agenda placed at each seat or a PowerPoint (or equivalent) presentation can help keep you on track. Don't try to fill every minute. Be confident the conversation will keep the meeting momentum going.

Begin the meeting with a short introduction about your organization and why you have gathered people together. You may want to ask attendees to complete a survey prior to your meeting to use as a springboard for discussion. This step allows you to get baseline opinions that have not been biased by other attendees' ideas. Alternatively, share the results of a larger community survey and ask them to comment on it.

Intersperse group discussion with opportunities to get people out of their seats. For example, instead of just asking people to describe your organization, hang large pieces of paper with different adjectives written on each around the room. Invite people to walk around the room and choose the ones that best describe your organization by marking them with a star or check. After five minutes, discuss their choices.

Similarly, if you are looking for feedback on a name or logo, place images of your top choices on a table with a jar or bowl next to each image. Give attendees something to vote with—pennies, pencils, straws—and instruct them to select the one or two they like the best. Once their selections are made, ask why they chose the ones they did (or didn't) to gain an insight on what each option conveyed to the attendees.

Wrap up the meeting by thanking attendees and telling them how you will be following up with them either individually or as a group.

One-on-One Interviews

Rather than convening a group, the Moab Museum conducted a four-month community assessment through thirty-five one-on-one interviews. The impetus for the community assessment, recalls Forrest, was the plan to build a large, new natural history museum and "bring home" geological and archeological artifacts now in the collections of big museums like the Peabody and the American Museum of Natural History.[6]

"I asked the Board, is this new museum just two peoples' dream? What does the community want?" The board, comprised primarily of people interested in natural history, tasked Forrest with asking the community.

"The assessment looked at community attitudes and perceptions," he recalls. "It focused on one essential element of the original idea, which was to establish the museum as a certified federal repository that would allow it to retain archeological and paleontological objects."

The recommendations from the community assessment led the museum in a different direction. "Don't build a building, build an organization," says Forrest, reciting the key takeaways from the assessment. "Revitalize the visitor experience. Be more effective in engaging the community because that's going to be required for you to build memberships, local community support, and advocacy."

"We used the community assessment as the blueprint for moving forward," says Forrest. "The rebranding activity grew out of that. Fortunately, the board recognized we were creating something that was completely new to the community."

Begin by identifying what you want to learn from the interviews and whom you need to interview to obtain that information. You may be interested in something as broad as audience perception or as focused as a name or logo choice.

Develop a questionnaire an interviewer can follow but that is loose enough so the interviewer can react to a response. To get the conversation flowing, open the interview with a few simple, easy-to-answer questions such as how long they have lived in town or how many times they have visited your site. As you get into the heart of the interview, start broadly and move to more focused questions. Questions for one-on-one interviews could include:

- Have you ever visited our site? If so, when?
- How was your experience?
- Would you recommend it to a friend? Why or why not?
- What needs do you think our organization fills in the community? Is the community-at-large aware of that?
- How does our organization differ from similar local, regional, state-wide organizations?
- Did you know that we offer X, Y, and Z?
- How aware do you think the community is of our resources?
- How do you think the community perceives our organization?
- When you hear our name, what do you think of? (Or, when you hear "historical society," what do you think of?)
- Which of these three logos best captures what our organization is? Why?

Also remember to collect age, gender, race, ethnicity, and education level, as you may notice a trend emerge during the interview process.

Decide who will conduct the interviews. Interviewers should be non-biased (or at least appear that way) and, if the interview is going to be in-depth and exploratory, intimately familiar with the topic so they are comfortable reacting to responses. An executive director, CEO, or a hands-on board member is a natural choice in a small organization. Larger organizations may have a dedicated market research team who could conduct the interviews.

One benefit of one-on-one interviews is flexibility. Rebranding efforts at the Virginia Museum of History and Culture led to one-on-one interviews with other museum directors and leaders in the cultural sector regionally and across the state.The Pejepscot History Center Board interviewed key stakeholders, major donors, and other board members as part of their market research, particularly delving into "must haves" and "must not haves" associated with the name.[8] At the Northwest Montana History Museum, Jacob explored logo options with a handful of people in what he refers to as "an informal vetting." The Montclair History Center also vetted its name and potential logos informally, making sure to include younger staff members and interns in its sampling.

Several organizations used one-on-one interviews to help communicate the need to rebrand. "We did one-on-one meetings with stakeholder groups leading up to the change," recalls Jamison. "We talked to several people in the Ohio House and Senate and the Governor's office just to make sure they understood and were informed." They also reviewed the market research data individually with board members, objectively demonstrating the need for a change. As Jamison says, "The proof was there."

QUANTITATIVE RESEARCH

Surveys

Surveys are the simplest way to add hard numbers to your market research. A survey can be completed online, via phone or direct mail, or in person.

While there is a science behind creating a survey, and professionals may spend months perfecting a questionnaire before fielding it, you can create and complete an online survey easily and inexpensively. Several websites offer online surveys—Pollfish, QuestionPro, SurveyMonkey, SurveyPlanet, and Typeform—to name just a few. Most have similar features: survey creation, survey templates, and tools to analyze data. They all have different pay structures. Many have a free model with a limited number of responses and features but the ability to pay for additional responses and features.

As you design your survey, keep the following guidelines in mind:

- Aim for simple questions. Multiple choice, select all that apply, yes/no, and true/false questions are easiest to analyze once your responses are in. You can always add a final open-ended question or two for other comments.
- Make sure you are asking only one question at a time. "When you arrived at the museum, were you greeted warmly and on a timely basis?" is actually two questions—one about the quality of interaction and one about wait time.
- Eliminate leading questions or verbiage. For example, "Please rate our award-winning tour on a scale of 1 to 5."
- Be aware that how you ask questions and the order can unintentionally bias responses. The open-ended question, "What's the first word you think of when you hear the name of our organization?" will likely yield different answers than if you ask people to select adjectives from a list, even if that list is balanced with positive and negative answers. If you choose to ask both, ask the open-ended question first because your preselected list will influence responses. Similarly, if you want to

determine awareness of a specific program, exhibit, or resource, make sure you haven't mentioned it in a prior question.

- Keep it short. To determine how long people are willing to spend on a survey, researchers at SurveyMonkey analyzed people's interactions with 100,000 surveys of varying lengths. They found people spent more time answering each question in shorter surveys and that "abandon rates" (i.e., they left the survey unfinished) increased if surveys took more than seven to eight minutes to complete.[9]
- Ask questions about the respondents' demographics. At a minimum, include questions about age and gender. You may also want to know where they live, how long they have lived there, distance from the site, race and/or ethnicity, and level of education.
- Test it before you field it. Complete the survey yourself first; then pass it to a few colleagues or family members for feedback. A fresh set of eyes can help you make sure your questions are clear and unambiguous.

The number of people to survey is also a science, although most small organizations are often just thankful to get a decent number of responses. Back in 2010, when HistoryMiami hired a Boston-based branding company, consultants surveyed people to find out if they knew the museum and what types of exhibits interested them. Although Jorge was not involved with the process, he recalls a lot of conversation about sample size. "It was a very small sampling . . . 100 people representing 2.5 million people in Miami. But it's what you can afford. The services are expensive."[10] Experts say to aim for about 10 percent of the total population you are surveying, not to exceed 1,000 people, and the larger the number the more the accurate results. A good and usually affordable minimum sample size is 100.[11] To encourage people to participate, you may want to consider an incentive such as entering them in a drawing for a free gift or membership.

Next, determine how to field the survey. You can send it to your email list, but that will skew your results to people who know about your organization. If you want community responses in general, look for other ways to disseminate it, such as through online media or partner organizations' email lists and websites. If you promote it through social media, consider spending a little money to boost your post. You will reach a broader audience than your own direct followers. Some online survey companies have panels of paid responders, giving you the option to buy random responses to your questions. Although it requires more work, you may also want to send a printed version via regular mail, particularly if you want to include an audience you know is not tech savvy. When a hard copy is returned, enter it into the online computer survey tool to ensure these results are included in your analysis. You could also field the question in person, inviting people to complete the survey on a tablet.

Eighteen months before the Montclair History Center rebranding was introduced, the team fielded a survey to determine the public's perceptions about the Montclair Historical Society. They asked questions about the respondents' interest in local history, involvement in the organization, awareness about its sites and activities, and the most effective forms of communication.

They sent a survey link twice to an internal mailing list of approximately 2,000 people. Board members and staff invited their contacts to participate. The survey was also announced on the organization's website, the Montclair Business Improvement District's website, and a local news website. A total of 227 people responded, a good response rate.[12]

The results showed that people who were familiar with the Montclair Historical Society labeled it most frequently as "educational" and "interesting." However, a closer analysis of the data revealed that younger respondents who were less familiar with the organization labeled it as "tired," "out of touch," and "boring." Although they knew nothing about the organization other than its name, that was enough to elicit a strong negative reaction.

Pejepscot History Center also fielded a member survey to "better understand and define its role in the community." The fourteen-question survey explored whether active and former members believed the organization's mission is accurate and their opinion of the name "Pejepscot Historical Society." You can find the questions included in Montclair History Center's and Pejepscot History Center's survey questions at the end of this chapter.

To understand audience perceptions outside their own base, Jamie says the Virginia Museum of History and Culture "did some list-sharing with other museums and cultural organizations across the Commonwealth." Casting the net wide, as Jamie did, does not mean you can't focus in on a certain group. If, for example, you are interested in people within only a certain radius of your site or people who are interested in history, ask for that information early in the survey and terminate it when people don't meet the criteria.

Five Oaks used a small survey to elicit feedback on the three possible new names—Washington County Museum, Museum of the Tualatin Valley, and Five Oaks Museum. They emailed the three options to about fifty people who were on the board or were long-term members, friends of the museum, and museum colleagues. They didn't create an online survey; they simply asked for feedback. The co-directors wrote up and presented a summary of the responses to the board with representative comments for and against each choice. This exercise allowed the board to make an informed choice for a new name.[13]

You may also want to use in-person surveys as part of your research mix. While you can take your survey on a clipboard to a busy downtown location and ask people to stop and take a survey, depending on your goals, you may have more success with a captive audience. Consider asking visitors or program attendees. Remember, though, unless someone enters the responses into a tablet, in-person surveys require hand tabulation and are more labor intensive.

Phone Surveys

Phone surveys can generate immediate results and reach a broad audience, but unless you are calling targeted individuals who know you and will answer the phone, this type of research is best left to professionals. Market research companies that offer phone surveys use a system known as "CATI," or Computer Assisted Telephone Interviewing, that pops a phone number on a screen and leads a trained interviewer through a series of questions.

The cost depends on whether you are calling cell phones or landlines and whether the survey is automated or live. Live surveys to cell phone users may cost several thousands of dollars for a basic survey.[14,15,16]

Polls

A poll, like a survey, generates quantitative data. Unlike a survey, it generally consists of one or two questions and takes just seconds to complete.

When the Ohio History Connection was in the midst of rebranding, their market researcher wanted to solicit customer perceptions of the old and new name from parents with young children. She worked with a local zoo, where she knew she would find a target audience interested in family cultural activities. "She set her table outside one of the exhibits," says Jamison. "As people walked out, she would intercept them and say, 'Hey, would you mind doing a quick word association?' She would show them both names and a few of the descriptors they could apply to either." The results demonstrated people associated words like "dynamic" more with the Ohio History Connection than with the Ohio Historical Society.

Think of other places you can get quick feedback from a large group of people: a local fair or flea market, outside the train station, a high school football game, another organization's event, a park, or the town pool. Let's say you want the public's impression of three logos. You can simply approach people and ask which one appeals to them most. You can set up a table and invite people to drop a plastic coin, piece of candy, or some other object into an opaque can (so they are not influenced by others' choices) next to their favorite one. You can also use a polling app and invite people to answer questions on a tablet. Consider enticing people to participate with a small incentive.

DOCUMENT YOUR RESEARCH

After you've conducted your research, write up an analysis including the goals, audience, dates it was fielded, methodology, and results. You may want to use this analysis to support your efforts moving forward or to present to your board.

This information is also useful even if you just file it away. Twenty years from now, someone may come across this primary research and better understand the choices you made. As historians, we owe that to the next generation.

In this chapter, we talked about qualitative and quantitative research tools you can use to help determine the need for and the course of your rebranding. In chapter 4, we'll discuss changing the organization's name from a legal perspective. This process should be simultaneous to the design process so when you are ready to launch, you have all the legal paperwork filed, approved, and ready to go.

ASK YOURSELF

1. What do I need to know as we embark on our rebranding?
   a. Is it necessary? Why or why not?
   b. What is the current perception of my brand? Does it reflect what your organization is or has evolved into? Does it reflect your organization ten years ago? Will it reflect your organization ten years from now?
   c. Do you want feedback on a new name, look, vision, mission?
2. Which target audience can best provide that data?
   a. The public?
   b. People who know you (e.g., members, donors, visitors)?
   c. Funders?
   d. Board members?
   e. Other (e.g., government organizations)?
3. What is the best way to reach the target audiences? If you want responses from people outside your base, how can you engage them?
4. What is the best timing for the research?
   a. Before you begin, as baseline data?
   b. In midstream, for guidance on public response to different names and looks?
   c. At the end, to evaluate your efforts?
5. Will qualitative or quantitative research better meet my goals? Do I need both? Can I afford both?

6. What is my budget, if any, for research? How can I conduct research with limited or no budget?
    a. Is there a local agency that might be willing to provide pro bono services?
    b. Is there a local university that might be interested in helping conduct market research?
    c. Is there a donor who might be interested in funding a research project?
    d. Is there a low-cost option I can use to meet my goals? A small online survey, a community gathering, one-on-one interviews, a quick poll at a local event?
7. What does the research tell us?
    a. About how our organization is perceived as a whole? Does this differ by target audience?
    b. What do people think about current or future name or logo?
    c. What are our strengths? Growth opportunities? Areas for improvement?

MONTCLAIR HISTORY CENTER SAMPLE ONLINE SURVEY

How important is local history to you?

☐ Not important
☐ Moderately important
☐ Very important

Have you heard of:

☐ The Montclair Historical Society
☐ The Crane House and YWCA
☐ The Montclair Community Farm at the Montclair Historical Society
☐ I have not heard of any these

Have you ever been a member of the Montclair Historical Society?

☐ I am currently a member
☐ I have been a member in the past
☐ I have never been a member
☐ Don't know

Have you visited one of its sites or attended a program offered by the Montclair Historical Society?

☐ Never
☐ In the last year
☐ In the last five years
☐ More than five years ago
☐ What was most memorable?

What comes to mind when you hear "Montclair Historical Society"? Select all that apply.

☐ Crane House
☐ Family programs
☐ YWCA
☐ Historical Society's Research Library
☐ Programs for adults
☐ Herb sale
☐ Third grade field trip
☐ Old buildings
☐ Museum shop
☐ Hearth cooking
☐ Montclair Community Farm
☐ Children's programs
☐ Walking tours
☐ I am not familiar with the Montclair Historical Society
☐ Other (please specify)

What age group(s) do you think the Montclair Historical Society caters to most?

☐ Elementary school age
☐ Teenagers
☐ Families
☐ Adults
☐ Seniors
☐ Other (please specify)

What three words best describe the Montclair Historical Society?

☐ Relevant
☐ Tired
☐ Interesting
☐ Boring
☐ Creative
☐ Out of touch

☐ Fun
☐ Innovative
☐ Educational
☐ Progressive
☐ Don't know enough to answer
☐ Other (please specify)

What gender do you identify with?

☐ Male
☐ Female
☐ I'd prefer not to answer

What race/ethnicity do you consider yourself?

☐ White
☐ Black or African American
☐ American Indian or Alaskan Native
☐ Asian
☐ Native Hawaiian or other Pacific Islander
☐ From multiple races
☐ Some other race (please specify)

What is your age?

☐ 17 or younger
☐ 18–29
☐ 30–39
☐ 40–49
☐ 50–59
☐ 60 or older

What is your zip code?

☐ 07042
☐ 07043
☐ Other (Zip):

What topics are you interested in learning about?

☐ General history
☐ Genealogy
☐ Home restoration

☐ Architecture
☐ Historic preservation
☐ Gardening/farming
☐ Research on my home or neighborhood
☐ Other (please specify)

Which periods in American history are most interesting to you?

☐ All
☐ Precolonial (prior to 1620)
☐ Colonial (1620–1776)
☐ A Young America (1777–1850)
☐ Civil War and the Victorian Period (1850–1900)
☐ Early Twentieth Century (1900–1940)
☐ Civil Rights Era (1940–1970)
☐ Post 1970 to present day
☐ Other (please specify)

Where do you find out information about upcoming programs and events? Select all that apply.

☐ Emails from the organization
☐ Website
☐ Facebook
☐ Twitter
☐ *Montclair Times*
☐ *Star Ledger*
☐ *Suburban Essex*
☐ Baristanet
☐ Montclair Patch
☐ Tap into Montclair
☐ Word-of-mouth
☐ *Jersey Tomato Press*
☐ Other (please specify)

Please add my name to your email list (optional):

Thank you for your time!

PEJEPSCOT HISTORY CENTER SAMPLE ONLINE SURVEY

The Pejepscot Historical Society is embarking on an initiative to better understand and define its role in the community and to strengthen its work to preserve and present regional history. We invite you to help us with this initiative by completing this questionnaire. An understanding of your knowledge of PHS, what it is you would like to see PHS provide to you and the region, and the level of support for our efforts will be essential to our continued development and success.

When I hear the name Pejepscot Historical Society I think of . . . (Check all that apply.)

- ☐ Historical artifacts
- ☐ Museum exhibits
- ☐ Historical documents
- ☐ Programs
- ☐ Historical and genealogical research resource
- ☐ The Skolfield-Whittier House
- ☐ The Joshua L. Chamberlain House
- ☐ Education
- ☐ All the above
- ☐ None of the above

Other (Please specify) _____

The mission statement of the Pejepscot Historical Society is *The Pejepscot Historical Society preserves, interprets, and promotes the rich history of Brunswick, Topsham, and Harpswell, Maine, through its collections, programs, and historic house museums.*

Please select your understanding of this statement:

- ☐ This is exactly what I think PHS does.
- ☐ This is close to what I think PHS does.
- ☐ This is completely different from what I think PHS does.
- ☐ I have no knowledge of what PHS does.

How would you rank the importance of PHS to the quality of life and sense of place in the community:

- ☐ Very important
- ☐ Somewhat important
- ☐ Not important at all

The Pejepscot Historical Society is well known for providing:

(Check all that apply.)

- ☐ Local history education to children
- ☐ Local history education to adults and visitors
- ☐ Inspiration to people of all ages to learn more about the past
- ☐ A learning center through exhibits, research, and its collection and historic houses
- ☐ Education about how people lived and worked over time
- ☐ Historical insight into the lives of past members of the community
- ☐ A center where people can come together to celebrate its history and traditions
- ☐ Advocacy for historic preservation
- ☐ A sense of a shared past

Other (Please specify.)_____

The last time I visited any of the Pejepscot Historical Society sites was:

- ☐ Within the past year
- ☐ Within the past two years
- ☐ Longer than two years ago
- ☐ Never

When I last visited the Pejepscot Historical Society I was there to:

(Check all that apply.)

- ☐ Visit the Joshua L. Chamberlain Museum
- ☐ Visit the Skolfield-Whittier House
- ☐ Visit the museum exhibits
- ☐ Participate in a walking tour
- ☐ Attend a brown-bag lunch
- ☐ Do research—people, sites, buildings, events, genealogy, collection items, etc.
- ☐ Participate in a book group
- ☐ Learn what the Society had to offer
- ☐ Volunteer

In the past I have attended the following events sponsored by the Pejepscot Historical Society:

(Check all that apply.)

- ☐ Brown-bag lunch speaker
- ☐ History happy hour
- ☐ History walk tours
- ☐ Special exhibit opening
- ☐ Chamberlain Days
- ☐ Historical lecture
- ☐ Holiday member party
- ☐ Santa Day

Other (Please specify.)_____

I am a member of the Pejepscot Historical Society because:

(Check all that apply.)

- ☐ I enjoy learning about history.
- ☐ I enjoy learning about my community and its history.
- ☐ I like to support local organizations.
- ☐ The organization is important to the community and the region.
- ☐ I join for member benefits.
- ☐ I enjoy being a docent.
- ☐ I have skills and/or knowledge that I feel contributes to the Society's mission.
- ☐ I enjoy being part of an organization and meet new people.

I am not currently an active member of the Pejepscot Historical Society because:

(Check all that apply.)

- ☐ I do not know how to join.
- ☐ I am not aware of the benefits of membership.
- ☐ I already belong to too many organizations.
- ☐ I am not interested at this time.
- ☐ It's too expensive.
- ☐ I do not live in this region of the country.
- ☐ It's not of interest to me.
- ☐ I was a member but have not renewed because (Please specify.)

What kinds of programs, exhibits, or benefits would motivate you to visit or join the Pejepscot Historical Society? (Check all that apply.)

☐ Speaker on an historical topic, event, or person
☐ Speaker on a topic of local interest
☐ Speaker on current affairs
☐ Historical book talk by author
☐ Book discussion
☐ Special tours of exhibitions or the Society's collection
☐ In-depth opportunities to explore specific subjects, i.e., workshops, seminars, trips
☐ Children or student learning opportunities
☐ Reciprocal memberships or privileges with other similar organizations
☐ Program discounts
☐ Free research assistance
☐ Free house museum admission
☐ Other (Please specify.)

Have you ever visited the Pejepscot Historical Society's website or Facebook page?

☐ Website
☐ Facebook page
☐ I am not aware they exist

Is "Pejepscot Historical Society" the right name for the organization?

☐ Yes
☐ No
☐ I don't have an opinion.

If you answered yes or no, please tell us what it is about the name that you like or dislike.

Does the Pejepscot Historical Society logo fit the organization?

☐ Yes
☐ No
☐ I don't have an opinion.

If you answered yes or no, please tell us what it is about the logo that you like or dislike.

Please tell us about yourself: (Check all that apply.)

- ☐ Male
- ☐ Female
- ☐ Current member of PHS
- ☐ Docent at PHS
- ☐ Volunteer at PHS
- ☐ Student
- ☐ Parent of school-age children
- ☐ Employed
- ☐ Retired

Residency

- ☐ Resident of Topsham
- ☐ Resident of Harpswell
- ☐ Resident of Brunswick
- ☐ Resident of other local community (zip code_____)
- ☐ Seasonal resident
- ☐ Visitor (zip code_____)

Age

- ☐ Under 19
- ☐ 19–25
- ☐ 26–45
- ☐ 46–65
- ☐ Over 65

Are there other thoughts, comments, or suggestions you would like to share with us?

Thank you very much for sharing your thoughts and impressions of the Pejepscot Historical Society. Your feedback and suggestions are very important to us as we plan the future of the Society.

NOTES

1. Jamie Bosket (chief executive officer) in discussion with the author, June 2020.
2. Jacob Thomas (executive director) in discussion with the author, May 2020.

3. "What Is a Focus Group and What Do They Cost?" *Small Business Trends*, accessed December 15, 2020, https://smallbiztrends.com/2020/07/what-is-a-focus-group.html.

4. Jamison Pack (chief marketing officer) in discussion with the author, May 2020.

5. Elizabeth Hynes (president, board of trustees) in discussion with the author, October 2020.

6. Forrest Rogers (interim executive director) in discussion with the author, July 2020.

7. Larissa Vigue Picard (executive director) in discussion with the author, May 2020.

8. "How Much Time Are Respondents Willing to Spend on Your Survey?" SurveyMonkey, accessed January 2, 2021, https://www.surveymonkey.com/curiosity/survey_completion_times/.

9. Jorge Zamanillo (executive director) in discussion with the author, July 2020.

10. "How to Choose a Sample Size (for the Statistically Challenged)," Tool4dev.com, accessed December 30, 2020, http://www.tools4dev.org/resources/how-to-choose-a-sample-size/.

11. Jane Eliasof, "Market Research Survey Analysis for the Montclair Historical Society," unpublished report, June 2015.

12. Molly Alloy (co-director) in discussion with the author, May 2020.

13. Thomas Guterbock, Grant Benson, and Paul Lavrakas, "The Changing Costs of Random Digital Dial Cell Phone and Landline Interviewing," *Survey Practice* 11, no 2 (March 2018), https://www.surveypractice.org/article/3168-the-changing-costs-of-random-digital-dial-cell-phone-and-landline-interviewing.

14. "Collecting Survey Data," Pew Research Center, accessed December 29, 2020, https://www.pewresearch.org/methods/u-s-survey-research/collecting-survey-data/.

15. "Automated Voice Recorded Voter Opinion Surveys: The Good and the Bad," accessed December 29, 2020, https://magellanstrategies.com/automated-voice-recorded-surveys/.

CHAPTER 4

Making It Legal

After much discussion, some research, and perhaps a bit of trepidation, you may have decided the rebranding should include a new name. If so, it's time to make it legal. Start the process as soon as you've formally agreed on a new name. You'll want the legal paperwork in place by the time you go live with your new brand.

To adopt a new name for your organization, you can choose either of two routes:

- Legally rename your organization. Your organization's legal name is the one on its articles of incorporation and bylaws, the Form 990 you file annually with the IRS, and on many grant applications. Under this scenario, the old organization name ceases to exist as a business entity.
- Adopt a "DBA" or "Doing Business As" name. The old and new names legally coexist. Your organization preserves the original name, but you are free to use the new name on letterhead, marketing materials, fundraising, banking, etc. You may also hear this option referred to as a "trade name," "fictitious business name," or "assumed name."

Under both scenarios, your organization retains both its existing 501(c)(3) nonprofit designation and its Employer Identification Number (EIN), the nine-digit number the IRS uses to identify business tax accounts.

In this chapter, your colleagues share their thoughts about the two different options, including rationale for their choices and pros and cons of each. This chapter also provides you with general steps to follow for each option. Please keep in mind, each state has different requirements. Do some research about your state's requirements and speak with an attorney before you begin.

DBA OR LEGAL NAME CHANGE?

Having a dual name is as old as historic preservation in the United States. The Mount Vernon Ladies' Association of the Union, the first national historical preservation organization founded in 1853, owns and operates the historic site known as George Washington's Mount Vernon.[1] Most visitors likely have no idea that "George Washington's Mount Vernon" is a trade name.

The Virginia Museum of History and Culture has a similar construct. "We created a brand hierarchy," explains Jamie Bosket. "Technically, Virginia Historical Society is our legal identity and the identity our board of trustees operates under. The Virginia Museum of History and Culture—the place to visit—is owned and operated by the Virginia Historical Society."[2]

The decision to retain the Virginia History Society name was due, in part, to a desire to preserve a historical identity that dates to 1831. Having a legal identity and a promotional or brand identity also allowed them to ease into the new name. Says Jamie, "For a period of about eighteen months after launch, all of our member communications had to have both names, to emphasize that the organization Virginia Historical Society still exists and the place to visit is the Virginia Museum of History and Culture."

At first, the Virginia Historical Society seal remained prominent on letterhead that went to members. Then the seal disappeared, and the Virginia Museum of History and Culture name was placed above Virginia Historical Society. The old name, however, was always referenced in the text. Finally, the Virginia Historical Society was removed entirely unless it specifically referred to the operating organization.

Although not nearly as old as the Virginia Historical Society, the Montclair Historical Society was celebrating its fiftieth anniversary when its leadership was considering a name change. While many of the founders and original members had moved, were no longer active, or had passed away, there was still a core group who identified with the Montclair Historical Society. "By retaining the name," says Elizabeth Hynes, "we retained the history. With the DBA name, we were able to reimagine our brand for a new, more diverse, and often younger audience."[3]

Most of the organizations featured in *Rebranding: A Guide for Historic Houses, Museums, Sites, and Organizations* are operating with a DBA name rather than a new legal name:

- The Ames Historical Society is doing business as the Ames History Museum.[4]
- The Historical Association of Southern Florida, Inc., is doing business as HistoryMiami Museum.[5]
- The Southeastern Utah Society of Arts and Sciences is doing business as the Moab Museum.[6]

- The Montclair Historical Society is doing business as the Montclair History Center.
- The Northwest Montana Historical Society, Inc., is doing business as the Northwest Montana History Museum.[7]
- The Pejepscot Historical Society is doing business as Pejepscot History Center.[8]
- The Virginia Historical Society is doing business as the Virginia Museum of History and Culture.

Most of the leaders at these organizations are comfortable with their decisions to file a DBA rather than legally changing the name. Like their colleagues at the Virginia Museum of History and Culture and the Montclair History Center, they believed the DBA process in their state was more simple than a legal name change and/or it kept the legacy of the old name alive.

Jamison Pack at the Ohio History Connection has a different opinion. The Ohio Historical Society was doing business as the Ohio History Connection for six years before officially voting to embrace Ohio History Connection fully. "That proved challenging to us," she says. "As a collecting institution, we have paperwork for six years as the Ohio Historical Society DBA Ohio History Connection." She also notes that because funders want organizations to use a legal name when applying for grants, it can be confusing. Finally, she says, "Our staff needs full permission, full empowerment, to use the new name in order for it to be fully recognized and adopted." In hindsight, she says she would have gone about the rebranding differently and lobbied for a complete legal name change.[9]

Donna Odom at SHARE didn't hesitate about legally changing the organization's name. She was eager to shed the old name. "Nobody could ever remember Southwest Michigan Black Heritage Society," recalls Donna. "And there was no way to use an acronym."[10] For Donna, there was no going back. A legal name change made sense and the Society for History and Racial Equity, or SHARE, was born.

Judy Zulfiqar says the Southern California Railway Museum was the legal name, but at the time of the rebranding the organization was operating under a different name—Orange Empire Railway Museum. They rebranded by embracing what was already the organization's legal name.[11]

The First Americans Museum was originally conceived as the Native American Cultural and Educational Authority. According to its website, "The museum originated as a project of the State of Oklahoma and was completed through a partnership between the State of Oklahoma and The City of Oklahoma City, with help of a Chickasaw Nation subsidiary, the American Indian Cultural Center Foundation, and numerous donors."[12] Leadership changed the museum name prior to opening. "In time, the American Indian Cultural Center Foundation will change its name to be consistent with the branding," says Shoshana Wasserman, "but there's such a web of relationships it would create more chaos right now prior to opening."[13]

Choosing a fictitious name or a legal name change is up to the organization's leadership. Neither option is inherently better than the other. Textbox 4.1 outlines the pros and cons of each choice.

TEXTBOX 4.1.   LEGAL NAME CHANGE OR DBA?

	Pros	Cons
Changing the name legally	• Clean break with the old name. • Once you have changed the name, it is done. You don't need to think about renewals.	• Loses the heritage of the original name. • May alienate long-time donors and members.
Filing for a DBA name	• Allows you to retain the heritage of the original name. • Helps people resistant to the change realize the old organization still exists. • Depending on your state requirements, it may be a simple process.	• Can be confusing to have a dual identity. • The staff and the public may be less likely to embrace the new name fully. • May need to be renewed every five to ten years.

MAKING THE CHANGE

Once you know how you want to proceed, it is time to set the wheels in motion. Do some online research, consult an attorney and your accountant, and speak with your bank. States and banks have different requirements and procedures you will need to follow.

A Legal Name Change

"How to change the name?" says Donna with SHARE. "Now that I had to research, but there's a lot of information online." She also spoke with an attorney who had helped them set up the nonprofit years earlier. "We've never been able to have an attorney on retainer, but we did have a lawyer walk us through the process pro bono."

A legal name change must be filed at both the state and federal levels.[14] The steps below will guide you through the general process; however, talk with a lawyer or government agency to make sure you are correctly following the process in your state.

1. Confirm the state's requirements for naming nonprofit organizations and make sure the name you have chosen is not too similar to other companies in your state. Most of this information is available online on the state government website.
2. The board of trustees must approve the new name in a formal vote. Make sure to record their approval in the meeting minutes. Note that while the government requires a board vote, your organization may have more stringent requirements (e.g., a member vote, two-thirds majority). Follow the guidelines set forth in the documents that govern your organization.
3. Update your organization's articles of incorporation or association, constitution, bylaws, and other organizing documents with an amendment specifying the new name.
4. File the amendment with the state agency responsible for this type of change. Usually a simple internet search "how do I file a business name change in the state of XYZ?" will direct you to the right place.
5. Inform the Internal Revenue Service on your next annual filing (i.e., Form 990). You will need to provide documentation along with Form 990 or send it by letter or fax. The documentation requirements vary for different types of organizations. For example, if your organization is incorporated, you will need to send a copy of the amendment of the articles of incorporation and proof of the filing with the appropriate state agency. If you are unincorporated, you will need to send a copy of the amendment to the articles of association, constitution, or other organizing document, showing the effective date of the change and signed by at least two officers, trustees, or members. The IRS website clearly spells out what you need to send and how to send it.[15]
6. Because your organization's structure hasn't changed, its EIN number remains the same and your 501(c)(3) designation remains intact. You will need to request an updated IRS reaffirmation letter with the new name as proof of the organization's tax-exempt status.[16] Contact the

IRS's Exempt Organizations (EO) Determinations Office to request the letter.

7. Inform your bank about the name change so they can update your organization's accounts. All banks have different policies; however, many will allow you to deposit checks written to both the old and new names.
8. Depending on the timing of the rebranding rollout, you can now begin to use the new name, updating your website, marketing material, and social media.

Textbox 4.2 includes a checklist of these steps.

TEXTBOX 4.2.   CHECKLIST FOR A LEGAL NAME CHANGE

☐ Confirm the name with the state
☐ Approve name at board level
☐ Amend governing documents
☐ File change with the state
☐ Inform the IRS
☐ Request a reaffirmation letter from the IRS
☐ Notify your bank

A DBA FILING

"We got in touch with a local lawyer just to make sure we knew what we needed to do and what made the most sense," recalls Casie Vance at the Ames History Museum. "We filed a 'fictitious name resolution' with the state of Iowa. That's the extent of what we did legally to change it."

Unlike legally changing your organization's name, filing for a DBA, assumed name, trade name, or a fictitious name varies greatly state by state. In Iowa, as Casie discovered, all she needed to do was file an application and pay a $5 fee.

Your state may require any combination of the following:[17]

- State filing: Most states require you to file an application at the state level.
- County filing: Some states may require you to file at either the county or state level or both.
- Local filing: Those states that do not require state or county filing may require you to file at the local level.

- Application fee: The fee for an initial application varies from $5 to $200.[18]
- Publication: Some states require you to publish your new name in a newspaper or legal publication.
- Renewal: Some states require you to renew your DBA every five to ten years. The fee can vary from $5 to $100.[19]

In addition to your state requirements, there are several steps to take that are in common with legally changing your name:

- Check to ensure the new name is available and not too similar to other organization's names. You can find this information on your state website.
- Contact your bank and provide them with the DBA documentation, giving you the ability to deposit checks under both names.
- Notify the IRS about the name change. You can do this by checking the "name change" box on page one of Form 990 and including your DBA.
- Contact the IRS to request a reaffirmation letter that includes the fictitious name.

Finally, keep in mind your DBA is now part of your legal identity. Use your legal name followed by your DBA (e.g., Ames Historical Society dba Ames History Museum) on all contracts and legal documents.

The steps for filing a DBA are outlined in Textbox 4.3.

TEXTBOX 4.3. CHECKLIST FOR FILING A DBA

☐ Confirm the name with the state
☐ Research your state requirements
☐ Depending on state requirements, complete the following:
    ☐ File change with state
    ☐ File change with the county
    ☐ File change with local government
    ☐ Pay the application fee
    ☐ Publish new name
☐ Inform the IRS on the next Form 990 you file
☐ Request a reaffirmation letter from the IRS
☐ Notify your bank

With the paperwork underway, it's time to dive into the fun part—designing a new look for your organization. In chapter 5, you'll discover how your colleagues created new logos, often on a shoestring budget.

ASK YOURSELF

As you decide whether to proceed with a legal name change or a DBA filing, consider the following questions:

1. Does your organization's old name convey a legacy you want to protect by retaining it? Does it have brand equity?
2. Will retaining the name, in addition to filing a DBA, satisfy your long-standing members and donors? Is that important to you?
3. Does your organization's old name carry any negative perceptions?
4. Will having a dual name dilute your rebranding efforts? Among staff? The general public? If so, how will you address that?
5. How cumbersome is the DBA filing in your state?
6. Does a periodic DBA renewal pose any challenges to your organization?

NOTES

1. "Mount Vernon Ladies' Association," George Washington's Mount Vernon, accessed January 4, 2021, https://www.mountvernon.org/preservation/mount-vernon-ladies-association/.

2. Jamie Bosket (chief executive officer) in discussion with the author, June 2020.

3. Elizabeth D. Hynes (president, board of trustees) in discussion with the author, October 2020.

4. Casie Vance (executive director) in discussion with the author, May 2020.

5. Jorge Zamanillo (executive director) in discussion with the author, July 2020.

6. Forrest Rogers (interim executive director) in discussion with the author, July 2020.

7. Jacob Thomas (executive director) in discussion with the author, May 2020.

8. Larissa Vigue Picard (executive director) in discussion with the author, May 2020.

9. Jamison Pack (chief marketing officer) in discussion with the author, May 2020.

10. Donna Odom (executive director) in discussion with the author, May 2020.

11. Judy Zulfiqar (chief strategist, Watermark Associates) in discussion with the author, August 2020.

12. "FAQ," First Americans Museum, accessed January 7, 2021, https://famok.org/faq/.

13. Shoshana Wasserman (deputy director) in discussion with the author, July 2020.

14. "How to Change a 501(c)(3) Corporation's Name," Legalzoom.com, accessed January 7, 2021, https://info.legalzoom.com/article/how-change-501c3-corporations-name.

15. "Change of Name—Exempt Organizations," Internal Revenue Service, accessed January 7, 2020, https://www.irs.gov/charities-non-profits/charitable-organizations/change-of-name-exempt-organizations.

16. "Do You Need a New EIN?" Internal Revenue Service, accessed January 7, 2021, https://www.irs.gov/businesses/small-businesses-self-employed/do-you-need-a-new-ein.

17. "Doing Business Under a Fictitious Name," Harbor Compliance, accessed January 7, 2021, https://www.harborcompliance.com/information/doing-business-under-a-fictitious-name.

18. "Doing Business Under a Fictitious Name," Harbor Compliance, accessed January 7, 2021, https://www.harborcompliance.com/information/doing-business-under-a-fictitious-name.

19. "Doing Business Under a Fictitious Name," Harbor Compliance, accessed January 7, 2021, https://www.harborcompliance.com/information/doing-business-under-a-fictitious-name.

CHAPTER 5

The Design Process

Now for the fun part. How can you convey your new brand to the world? As you will see in this chapter, your colleagues went about rebranding in different ways, but they all followed roughly the same path. They identified a graphic designer or design team, provided the designer with input about what they were looking for, worked with the designer to develop a logo they felt represented their organization, and presented it to the people within the organization who needed to sign off on it. If any market research was conducted to test the logos, it was done informally among staff, board, trusted volunteers, and family members.

In this chapter, we'll walk through how each team created a look they believe encapsulates their organization. Their collective wisdom is summarized at the end of this chapter.

AMES HISTORY MUSEUM

Casie Vance and the board wanted to stay local—very local. They selected Rippke Design, a company that had recently rebranded the Ames Main Street organization and was right across the street from their museum.[1]

"It was a really quick process," Casie recalls. "I met with them and talked about what we were looking for." Their old logo had "Ames Historical Society" in a cursive typeface, stacked on a brown background, as shown in figure 5.1.

They couldn't easily size it down because the words became too small to read. They were also concerned the old logo looked dated and didn't appeal to a younger audience.

"Three or four weeks later, they came back with ten options, which was a lot," says Casie. The staff members discussed the options. The board presi-

Ames Historical Society

AMES • IOWA

WWW.AMESHISTORY.ORG

Figure 5.1. The Ames Historical Society's former logo had white cursive letters on a chocolate brown background and was dated. Ames History Center.

dent and a member who had advocated for a change weighed in. Casie also reached out to a couple of former staff members and volunteers.

Based on those discussions, they identified their first choice. "Some of the others were more traditional, but this one embodied what we were looking for as far as attracting families and being more accessible and exciting," she says. Although there were a wide range of opinions about the ten options, everyone had a positive reaction to the one they settled on.

Casie worked with the design firm, tweaking the colors, and then presented their choice to the board. "I had the other nine logos in my back pocket," she recalls, "but everyone said they liked this one, so this was the one."

AMES HISTORY **MUSEUM**

Figure 5.2. The Ames History Museum's new logo has brighter colors—teal, orange, and red. The interplay of straight and curved lines give it a dynamic feel. Ames History Center.

The new logo, shown in figure 5.2, is a dynamic design with the initials "AHM" in teal, orange, and red with curves and straight lines intertwined in a distinct font. The logo can be placed horizontally with the words "Ames History Museum" to the right or vertically with the words below the initials. The word "museum" is bolded for emphasis. The colors and the combination of curves and straight lines are carried through as design features on their website, in marketing material, and in the museum, following a brand guide the design firm provided at the end of the process.

FIRST AMERICANS MUSEUM

"Coming out of the gate as a new museum, our branding had to be on point," says Shoshana Wasserman. While they knew the name America Indian Cultural Center and Museum wasn't going to work, they had a tribal graphic symbol in their logo they wanted to keep, shown in figure 5.3.[2] It had been designed by LaPlaca Cohen in New York, a firm that had designed iconic logos for the Museum of Modern Art, the Frank Lloyd Wright Foundation, and the Kennedy Center.[3]

Figure 5.3. The colors in the American Indian Culture Center and Museum's former logo symbolize the earth, sky, and sun. First Americans Museum.

The circular image was embedded with symbolism. Imagine the museum is at the center of the circle. Thirty-nine lines emanate from that center point, representing where the tribal nations are located today, as shown in figure 5.4. "It speaks to the museum's relationship with the tribes and is inclusive," says Shoshana. They also wanted to retain the bright symbolism of the color palette with the blue for sky, red for the red earth, and yellow for the sun or the dawning of a new day, while adding some vibrancy to the new color palette.

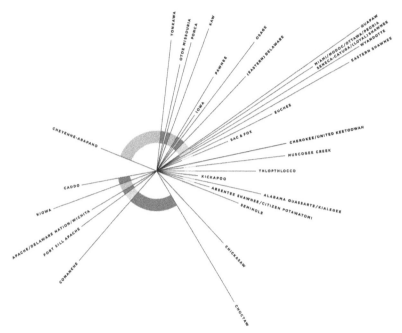

Figure 5.4. The radiating lines represent the locaton of the tribal nations. First Americans Museum.

The circle itself is also symbolic. "As native peoples, we look at time in cycles and circles," explains Shoshana. "We do not look at time in a linear fashion." This idea is carried throughout the whole museum, including its circular architectural design.

When they decided to change the name to First American Museum, they engaged Brand Navigation, whose principal and creative director, Bill Chiaravalle, co-wrote *Branding for Dummies*.[4] Brand Navigation designed a logo for the new name that uses geometric motifs, which are embedded in native cultural arts, shown in figure 5.5.

Figure 5.5. The First Americans Museum's new logo is playful, emphasizing "FAM" and embedded with geometric motifs common in First American cultural arts. First Americans Museum.

Rather than retire the circular symbol, they modified it and began to use it as a graphic element in their branding. Distinct from the FAM logo, it is nonetheless important to their brand and brand imagery, as shown in figures 5.6 and 5.7.

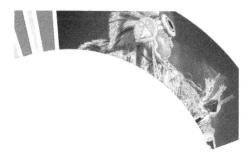

Figure 5.6. The former circular logo is now used as a graphic element in FAM's branding. Images may appear within the widened circle. First Americans Museum.

Figure 5.7. Or, images and videos fill the circular graphic element. First Americans Museum.

Shoshana noted many of the tribal nations have museums dedicated to their cultures. First Americans Museum also adopted a tagline, "One Place, Many Nations" to communicate that the museum represents all thirty-nine tribal nations in Oklahoma today.

The new branding went live at a press conference that featured a short, playful brand video introducing the new name, logo, and color palette. They animated the circular graphic element and integrated it with vibrant images of Oklahoma's First Americans. This video is housed on their website.[5]

"For native peoples," says Shoshana, "design motifs are encoded with storytelling. This is a contemporary way to carry on traditions we've had for generations."

First Americans Museum is also the only logo among those featured in *Rebranding: A Guide for Historic Houses, Museums, Sites, and Organizations* that bears a trademark. Legally trademarking your logo, name, tagline, or any combination distinguishes it from the competition. You can find out more about trademarking on the government's patent and trademark website, www.uspto.gov. They "strongly encourage you to hire [an attorney] who specializes in trademark law to guide you through the application process." Recognizing that this may make trademarking less appealing to small businesses, they also provide resources for pro bono legal support.[6]

FIVE OAKS MUSEUM

As they finalized a name, co-directors Molly Alloy and Nathanael Andreini began assembling a team to design their logo and website. A major donor had given a gift for the rebrand along with a recommendation for Roger That, a local branding and digital design company. Molly had met with them before becoming a co-director and called them a year-and-a-half later. Roger That was in sync with the museum's new direction and even honored an older bid, though the scope of the work had changed. Roger That's team began working on the website design.

As Molly and Nathanael began their search for a logo designer, they turned to LinkedIn. Because they both come from art backgrounds, their LinkedIn accounts were filled with designers. "We reached out to a few people whose portfolios resonated with us," says Molly.[7] They landed on Malini Gupta with Ochre {art + design} LLC. "Some designers have a style they just apply to every brand. Her style was fresh and robust. It felt like each brand belonged to the recipient." Malini was also willing to take on a collaborative approach and share design authority with Molly and Nathanael.

With the design team in place, it was time to start designing a logo for Five Oaks Museum that would replace the one for Washington County Museum, shown in figure 5.8.

Figure 5.8. The Washington County Museum's logo predates the orgaanaization's name change to Five Oaks Museum. Five Oaks Museum.

"We wanted something that harkened toward a modern art museum with a crisp, punchy aesthetic to it," says Molly, explaining the logo, shown in figure 5.9. "The logo is a five on its side. You can remove the "Five Oaks Museum" text and use it as a geometric stamp.

Figure 5.9. Five Oaks Museum's logo uses brown for the earth and periwinkle for the camas flower, an important native food anad plant to the region. Five Oaks Museum.

The logo symbolizes the oak tree that gave the museum its name. "The vertical line represents the trunk, the arch represents the canopy, and the block underneath the name represents the roots," continues Molly. "Those three elements of the oak tree have strong metaphoric meaning as far as being sturdy, creating a place of shelter and gathering, and being rooted in the community." Molly and Victoria Sundell, the museum's head of Integrated Learning, selected the colors themselves. The brown text for the name represents the earth, and the periwinkle represents the camas flower, an important native food and plant in this region.

The board entrusted Molly and Nathanael with the design process and execution. Once the co-directors were satisfied with the new design and website design, they could move ahead with implementing it across their promotional material.

HISTORYMIAMI MUSEUM

Back in 2010, when the Historical Museum of Southern Florida became HistoryMiami, the leadership team worked with BrandEquity, a design firm in Boston that created the logo shown in figure 5.10. When it was time for the refresh, they decided to do the work in-house. It helped that they had a strong marketing department and a good graphic designer on staff.

Figure 5.10. HistoryMiami's former logo was almost ten years old and ready for a refresh. HistoryMiami Museum.

The first thing their marketing director, Michele Reese Granger, did was slip the word "museum" into the existing logo. "We did that without a change of color or logo and let that sit for a few months," explains Michele. Then, it came time to address the color, which, says Michele, "wasn't reflective of Miami. Miami is bold. Miami is bright. Miami is diverse." The "cinnamon," as she calls it, didn't convey that.[8]

Because Miami is known for its turquoise waters, the team started there. "I don't think there's a more iconic color to contrast with it than pink," she says. It didn't hurt that their largest annual fundraiser is a Flamingo Ball.

Michele and her team had already embraced the values of inclusion, diversity, equity, and access (IDEA), a movement aimed at minimizing bias and reducing systemic inequalities that put some individuals or groups at a disadvantage. "This is the first time I had been part of a rebrand where accessibility took the forefront," she says.

Her team reviewed the design guidelines on the Americans with Disabilities Act website (ADA.gov). They also took advantage of free websites where you can test color choices against different backgrounds to ensure the contrast is great enough for easy readability. "We kept adjusting the color little by little until we found shades where the pink and the turquoise contrasted well on white and black backgrounds." There are similar websites where you can check how accessible your website and PDF files are. They traded HISTORYMIAMI in all caps for HistoryMiami in upper- and lowercase letters because it's easier to read. All marketing materials are now set in twelve-point type or larger. Their new logo is shown in figures 5.11 and 5.12.

HistoryMiami Museum

Figure 5.11 and 5.12. HistoryMiami Museum's new logo is teal and pink, bold and vibrant colors often associated with Miami. HistoryMiami Museum.

 HistoryMiami Museum

The final component of their branding, not visible in their logo, is putting people at the center of the brand. Most of the photos they use feature people. "What makes Miami special," explains Michele, "is that we are a vibrant, bold, incredible community filled with people from all over. We want people to see themselves in our museum, get inspired, and feel that sense of place."

MOAB MUSEUM

To develop a brand identity, Forrest Rogers called on Renate, a Portland-based agency "founded to rethink the relationship between institutions and community, to create systems that deepen creative collaboration, and to discover more meaningful ways of sharing stories."[9] Renate specializes in cultural institutions, museums, and science centers. He worked with the firm's principal to develop a questionnaire that he circulated to the board. The questions asked about the goals of the organization, the purpose, the audience, strengths, and weaknesses. For example:

- Why do you want a new, refreshed brand?
- Where do you see the institution in five years? Ten years? Thirty years?
- Who will be involved in the process and at what points?
- What brands do you admire and why?[10]

The board reviewed the answers individually, then responded to the firm collectively. The firm took that information and summarized it in a brand report, or brand strategy.[11]

"The next step was looking at logos, taglines, and the application of the graphics," Forrest recalls. "They developed concepts for us. They showed us logos from other institutions in the general region of Utah, southwestern Colorado, and northern New Mexico."Because there are a lot of other non-profits in Moab, many with Moab in the names, they also provided a local comparison.

One of the items on the wish list for a new logo was something that translated well in a variety of settings, even black and white. The old logo, shown in figure 5.13, was complex and had limited uses. Plus, says, Forrest, it was difficult to decipher unless it was in color.

Figure 5.13.   The former logo of the Museum of Moab wasn't flexible in a variety of settings. Moab Museum.

"They provided us with three or four different logos and four or five possible taglines," says Forrest. "We vetted them through staff and a couple of people from the community."

The overwhelming favorite was a bold, stylized "M" with "Moab Museum," shown in figure 5.14. The logo can be used in any of the colors in the brand palette, as well as in white against a color background, giving them the flexibility they were looking for. The new tagline, which is often included as part of the logo, is "Small Museum. Big Stories." The tagline

Figure 5.14. The new Moab Museum logo can be used in a variety of colors, even transparent, to let a photo shine through. Moab Museum.

is adaptable as well. During the COVID-19 shutdown, their website said, "Small Museums—Closed. Big Stories—Online."

"The agency selected the fonts and the style. They recommended a writing style and graphic system," says Forrest. Once the guidelines were set, Forrest passed them along to two freelancers who were responsible for incorporating the new brand into the website and across all communications pieces.

MONTCLAIR HISTORY CENTER

One of the Montclair History Center Board members, Kathleen Powers, is a graphic designer. She helped shepherd the process from concept to implementation. Kathleen recommends beginning with a well-defined design brief, much like the Moab Museum brand report, to share with the design team you select.

"At the very least," she says, "it should state your target audience, your goals and objectives, and your organization's key challenges."[12] A more fleshed out document could include an overview and history of your organization, your organization's mission, information about other nonprofits and what their branding looks like, your budget, and your timeline. Having a written document provides grounding. As you debate different design choices, it gives you a constant against which you can evaluate each design.

The Montclair History Center's team chose to work with a small, local branding firm, FanBrandz, to replace their old logo, shown in figure 5.15.

They provided the firm with the design brief they had developed and discussed what they wanted in a new logo. The greatest desire was to look contemporary. "We didn't want to look like an old, dusty, historical society," recalls Kathleen.

Because people had been calling the organization the "Montclair Historical Society" for fifty years, they wanted the new name, Montclair History Center, to be the central focus of the new logo. They wanted to stay away

Figure 5.15. When the Montclair Historical Society retired its former name, the green, outdated logo was retired too. Montclair History Center.

from initials or abstract graphics that could detract from the name. The new logo, shown in figure 5.16, met those objectives.

The design firm presented several logos that staff and volunteers (particularly those in their twenties and thirties) considered. Working with the design firm, the team narrowed it down to three strong contenders. The board weighed in and the new logo was selected.

As they developed the brand guide, FanBrandz identified a font that worked well with the new logo. The downside was the font was not standard in word processing programs and had to be purchased and downloaded to every laptop and desktop to keep the look consistent. In hindsight, the

Figure 5.16. The Montclair History Center's new logo features the name in primary colors and can be used in a variety of formats. Montclair History Center.

Montclair History Center team would have worked with the design firm to identify a standard font that coordinated with the logo.

Kathleen, who has worked with countless logos in her years as a graphic designer, is pleased with the final design. "Our logo has a shape, which from a design perspective, is easier to hang on to and reproduce," she says. "A good logo creates its own sacred space, which our logo does."

NORTHWEST MONTANA HISTORY MUSEUM

"The design was the fun part," says Jacob Thomas. "We wanted something with a little more life, a little more color, and that was a little more contemporary" than the previous logo, shown in figure 5.17.[13]

Figure 5.17. The Museum at Central School's former name and logo didn't tell people what the museum was about. Northwest Montana History Museum.

Jacob had heard the Flathead Valley Community College's advanced design classes worked with local nonprofits to design logos. He and the board vice president met with the professor to explain the project, and she quickly agreed to help. The idea was that students would submit logo drafts, and at the end of the process, Jacob and the board vice president would pick a design and work with the student to fine-tune it.

"We sat down with the class of six or seven students to discuss the project and how we wanted to use our new name. Students toured the museum to get a better of idea of our organization. Then we just washed our hands of it," recalls Jacob. "We wanted to see what the students came up with."

The winning design met their criteria of having more life and color and being more contemporary, as shown in figure 5.18. "It was a fantastic design, but it had no connection to history," says Jacob. They modified the logo's color scheme to emulate one used in the Pendleton Woolen Mill's Glacier Park blanket. The colors are iconic in the Northwest, associated with the national parks, and have a history with fur trading and the Native American population.[14,15] To ensure they were not violating any trademark or copyright laws, Jacob reached out to Pendleton, which granted permission, providing they changed the indigo to black.

Figure 5.18. The new Northwest Montana History Museum's logo captures the feel of the natural parks near Kalispell. Northwest Montana History Museum.

After fine-tuning the logo, they showed it to a few friends and volunteers to get their first impressions of it. Next, they presented it to the board, along with a tagline "Where the past is present." With board approval, they were ready to launch.

OHIO HISTORY CONNECTION

Jamison Pack knew hiring a large agency for the logo design wasn't in her budget. She also knew if she were to find an agency that would do the work pro bono, her staff would be burdened with the heavy lift of the rollout. She began to assemble a freelance team that included a graphic designer and a two-person public relations firm.[16]

The graphic designer presented a first round of concepts, which Jamison and her staff whittled down. They chose to keep the flag that had been in the Ohio Historical Society's logo to maintain the legacy, seen in figure 5.19, but update it. "The previous flag was flat," says Jamison. "We wanted something that had movement and reflected the energy we were looking to build and create." The result, seen in figure 5.20, bears a striking resemblance to the former logo, but is dynamic, emphasizes the new name, and has brighter colors.

Figure 5.19 and 5.20. The Ohio History Connection retained the state flag from their old logo, but gave it more life to reflect the energy they were looking to create. Ohio History Connection.

Once the logo was approved, they developed a brand book that provides guidelines on how to use the new logo, fonts, colors, style, and voice. While a brand book or style guide is important to any organization, it is particularly important in larger organizations where many people are responsible for creating graphic images, copy, and other communications for the general public. By following a brand book, everyone is speaking with one voice and the brand remains consistent and cohesive. It ensures the writers' and designers' personalities fade to the background, allowing the brand personality to emerge. Sample pages from the brand book are included at the end of this chapter.

After the overall Ohio History Connection rebrand, Jamison began co-branding the sites in the Ohio History Connection's large network of historical sites. The branding guide has become increasingly more important as people from across the state begin incorporating the Ohio History Connection logo into their sites' collateral material, websites, and signage.

PEJEPSCOT HISTORY CENTER

Pejepscot Historical Society's old logo was based on a place. It depicted a cupola atop the Skolfield Whittier House, their offices and exhibit space, as seen in figure 5.21. "It's a recognizable, iconic building in town," says Larissa Vigue Picard. "But it didn't have anything to do with the Chamberlain Museum," the Society's second building.[17]

The board had agreed to rename the organization but didn't agree on next steps. Some believed they just needed a logo, others believed they needed to issue a request for proposal (RFP) to find the right agency to work with, and still others believed they needed to develop a full marketing

Figure 5.21. Pejepscot Historical Society's former logo featured an iconic cupola found on one of their sites. Pejepscot History Center.

campaign before introducing the brand. With a hard deadline in place to coincide with Maine's Bicentennial, they finally agreed to ask the graphic designer who worked on their newsletters to submit a few designs. "We had a great meeting with her," recalls Larissa. "She really understood what we were looking for, which was something abstract."

They still wanted the logo to be connected to a place, but they wanted the focus to shift from the cupola to the Androscoggin River that flows through the three communities. "We were interested in tying in the idea of history flowing," says Larissa. "There are no starting and ending points in history. It flows together." Larissa says they also wanted to visually represent the three towns whose history and culture are preserved and shared at the museum.

Finalizing the logo took longer than planned. In December 2019, they announced the name in the newsletter and social media, postponing the logo reveal until their March annual meeting. Working with the designer, they tweaked colors and curves, crafting a logo that flows like both the Androscoggin River and history and has three distinct components representing the three communities.

The new logo, shown in figures 5.22 and 5.23, has several iterations that can be used for different purposes. "The main logo includes the tagline 'Discover your place in time,'" explains Larissa. "We wanted to convey the flow of history and that everybody has a point or multiple points on that line."

Figure 5.22 and 5.23. In blue, green, and purple, the Pejepscot History Center's new logo conveys the flow of a nearby river and the flow of history. Pejepscot History Center.

SOCIETY FOR HISTORY AND RACIAL EQUITY (SHARE)

When Donna Odom founded the Southwest Michigan Black Heritage Society, she says, "We realized most of the information about this area's history would come from the descendants of the folks who lived the history. There wasn't anything in the history books."[18] The logo, as shown in figure 5.24, symbolized the family trees through which history had been preserved.

Figure 5.24. The Southwest Michigan Black Heritage Society relied on stories passed down through family trees to document history. Society for History and Racial Equity.

The tree was no longer as relevant when the organization's focus grew to include social justice. Although Donna admits she knew nothing about branding, she did know she needed a graphic artist. "I had met a couple of designers through the Kalamazoo Valley Museum. They were very creative and had done a lot of work for the museum, so we asked them to design a logo for us."

That's when Donna learned about rebranding. Donna told the designers about the organization, its dual mission, and how its future was evolving. "We wanted history to be prominent, but we wanted the flavor of social justice," recalls Donna.

The creative team came back with a concept, shown in figure 5.25, that Donna and the board were impressed with and liked because it codified their dual mission of history and racial equity. Coincidentally, their leased office space was in an H-shaped building.

Figure 5.25. The new name and logo clearly communicate the organization's dual mission. Society for History and Racial Equity.

Society For History And Racial Equity

S · H · A · R · E

According to Donna, they had been using a tagline of "Acknowledging the past, healing the present." The tagline has since evolved to succinctly reinforce the dual mission: "Celebrating Black history. Eliminating racism."

SOUTHERN CALIFORNIA RAILWAY MUSEUM

The Orange Empire Railway Museum's dual focus of trains and trolleys was reflected in its former logo, shown in figure 5.26. Although distinctive and colorful, the logo was busy and difficult to use when a simple black-and-white image was needed.

Figure 5.26. Orange Empire Railway Museum's former logo was difficult to use when a simple black-and-white image was needed. Southern California Railway Museum.

When the name changed, the museum's board decided to create a new logo rather than simply replace the words in the old logo. Although Watermark Associates handles their communications, the board selected outside designer Wade Abbas, the lead graphic designer at Creative Printing, to create the new logo, shown in figure 5.27.[19]

The new logo uses the same orange as in the previous logo, a tribute to the museum's former name. The train and trolley from the old logo have disappeared, replaced by a single set of tracks that lead the eye to the new name. A prominent feature of the logo is the train's "pilot" or "cowcatcher," located below the words "railway museum." The pilot, an iconic image

Figure 5.27. The new Southern California Railway Museum conjures up images of the glory days of rail and trolley travel. Southern California Railway Museum.

among train aficionados, is designed to push debris (and cows) from the tracks. As in the old logo, the emphasis is on the words "railway museum.[20]

Compared to the former logo, the new logo's color scheme is simple and reproduces well as a black-and-white image or dropped out in white against a dark background. Overall, it mimics an art deco train design, echoing the look of some of the trains in their collection.

TWO MISSISSIPPI MUSEUMS

The Mississippi Museum of History had been closed for more than a dozen years since Hurricane Katrina had torn the roof off in 2005. As a result, the Godwin Group, the designers tasked with creating logos for the Two Mississippi Museums, had a clean slate to work with. Just like the museum staff, they had to wrestle with the idea that the two side-by-side museums were independent yet worked together.

"The goal was to identify a museum facility with a shared entrance and common space that opens up to two distinct exhibition experiences," explains James "Jimbo" Harwell, the creative director for the Godwin Group. His team created a branding system with separate logos (or "marks") for each museum that can be united into one, as shown in figure 5.28. "By echoing the exterior architecture of the museums, these marks are unified, but also distinct and able to stand alone," he says, as shown in figures 5.29 and 5.30.[21]

The logo for the Museum of Mississippi History has traditional lines that echo the columns on the building's exterior, according to Jimbo. It also subtly evokes a row of books and uppercase letter "M." The logo for the Mississippi Civil Rights Museum is "designed to encourage conversation and contemplation" and "while the angles evoke signs of tension and struggle, bright 'rays of light' illuminate progress." These two logos join, just like the two museum spaces.

TWO
MISSISSIPPI
MUSEUMS

MUSEUM OF	MISSISSIPPI
MISSISSIPPI	**CIVIL RIGHTS**
HISTORY	MUSEUM

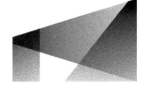

MUSEUM OF   MISSISSIPPI
MISSISSIPPI   **CIVIL RIGHTS**
HISTORY   MUSEUM

Figure 5.28, 5.29, and 5.30.   The Two Mississippi Museum's logo consists of two independent "marks" that come together as one. They may be used in combination or stand alone. Mississippi Department of Archives and History.

Recalling the day the Godwin Group presented their idea for the logo, Katie Blount says, "I thought, 'They nailed it.'"[22] Pamela Junior says, "I had to go outside and actually look at the buildings to understand it. It really shows the essence of the two buildings."[23]

Cindy Gardner was also part of that presentation. "I instantly got excited about it," she recalls. "The architect did a brilliant job of housing the history museum in a standard-looking government building that leads into the civil rights museum with modern lines. That the designer was able to bring that out in our logo sold it for me."[24]

Although the museums operate under the auspices of the State of Mississippi, they do have a strong independent board of directors. "We didn't take it to them for approval," say Katie, "but when we showed it to them, they loved it."

VIRGINIA MUSEUM OF HISTORY AND CULTURE

After deciding on a new name, Jamie Bosket says the next step was developing a creative look and feel, brand identity elements, new logo and style guide, and voice and brand language for the Virginia Museum of History and Culture. Although they would continue to use the Virginia Historical Society seal, seen in figure 5.31, the logo would be retired.

Figure 5.31. The former Virginia Historical Society logo. Virginia Museum of History and Culture.

"We used Love Affair Creative, the same small boutique marketing firm that helped us with the research," explains Jamie. "A lot of things were pretty obvious to us. We wanted bright vibrant colors, a more familiar voice, a little less formality, a little more relaxed spirit. Those things came naturally as we worked through what it was going to be."[25]

The creative designer brought several options, and the staff honed the choices from there. Over several meetings, they made their selection, shown in figures 5.32 and 5.33, and finalized the color palettes and fonts.

VIRGINIA MUSEUM OF HISTORY & CULTURE

Figure 5.32. and 5.33. The branding includes a logo and the museum's name and can be used alone or in combination. Virginia Museum of History and Culture.

The two elements—the graphic block and the name—may be used independently or together. Their website features the name, social media highlights the graphic, and their signage incorporates both.

COLLECTIVE WISDOM

As you begin designing your logo, take advantage of the collective wisdom and ideas from others who have gone through the process.

Step One: Identify the design team.

- Speak with a graphic designer you already work with.
- Review designers' portfolios and meet the ones whose logo designs appeal to you.
- Work with a local college.
- Stay local or choose to get a broader perspective by going further afield.
- Get recommendations from colleagues.
- Work with in-house talent.

Step Two: Tell the design team what you are looking for.

- Develop a document—a design brief, brand strategy, or brand report—to share with the design team.
- If the design team has a standard process for developing a brand look, give them the freedom to work through that process.
- Speak with them about the personality you want to project or symbolism you want to incorporate. Be patient. Sometimes, it takes several meetings before the designers truly understand what you are looking for.
- Tell them about how your old logo worked and didn't work for you.
- Let them know if the design will be static or if you want to be able to use variations for different applications.
- If your organization is the steward of more than one site, explore the possibility of co-branding within your organization. A designer can build in logo variations that relate to each site, just as the Ohio History Connection is doing with sites across the state and the Two Mississippi Museums did with their two distinct museums. Even if the organization is small, co-branding could help you establish its multiple sites are under the auspices of one organization.

Step Three: Collaborate with the design team.

- Let the design team design. That's what they are trained to do.
- Provide constructive feedback. Specifically, what do you like about a design? What don't you like? Why will it work? Why not? Let them find the creative solution to your concerns.
- Begin by focusing on design, not color. Color can be part of the fine-tuning process. Judy Zulfiqar of Watermark Associates says they

usually get buy-in on a black-and-white design before they introduce color.[26]

- Share a few of your top choices with staff, board, trusted volunteers, family, or friends to get their impression of the designs. Remember to include people who are part of the target audience you want to appeal to.
- Go back to your design brief. Does the logo satisfy those requirements?
- Assess how the logo variations will be used across applications—on a brochure, enlarged on a banner, as a small circular social media badge, on your website, etc.
- Check your new logo to see if it meets accessibility design standards using one of the many online tools available. There are also ones that can check your website and PDFs for contrast, font size, and other accessibility features. To find these services, search "check color contrast of website (or PDF) for accessibility" online.
- Once you've agreed upon a final design, make sure the design team develops a brand guide that at a minimum includes high resolution variations on the main logo and how the logo can be used, fonts, and colors. Ask for the Pantone (Pantone Matching System) color numbers as well as CMYK (cyan, magenta, yellow, black) percentages so you can input them into your software programs. This allows you to properly brand documents internally. Your brand guide can also include tone of voice (e.g., formal vs. informal) and brand language (e.g., if you should use "the" before your name). Sample pages from the Ohio History Connection's and Northwest Montana History Museum's brand guides are shown in figures 5.34 through 5.40 at the end of this chapter.

Step Four: Get the approvals you need to launch.

- Determine in advance who needs to formally approve the final logo choice.
- Decide what you mean by "approval." Is it a rubber stamp or do you want them to be actively involved in selecting the logo? You can show them:
  - Your final choice only
  - Your final choice but have others to show just in case they don't like it
  - Let them decide among the top few choices. Hint: Make sure you are okay with any you present.

Once the logo is designed and approved, don't look back and second-guess your choice. It's time to reveal it to the public.

BRAND BOOK SAMPLES

SECTION 7

Logo Usage

The official Ohio History Connection logo comprises a waving flag and the Ohio History Connection name. Consistent and appropriate use of the logo is required on all materials.

STANDARD LOGO	ONE-COLOR LOGO	REVERSED LOGO

This should be used as the primary logo option and always appear on white or a white value.

This should be used when **only one color is permitted**. Appropriate one-color options are black at 100% or dark blue at 100%; also white on a gray, light blue, medium blue or dark blue ground. *(See the three Primary Palette blues and the gray on p. 40.)* Other one-color options must be approved before use. The one-color logo is never screened in whole or in part.

This logo should be used when the logo appears on a non-white value. A white outline appears around the flag and the text is white.

FILE ACCESS

All logo files are available in .eps, .pdf and .png file formats. To request the official logo, please contact Mallory Skrobot at mskrobot@ohiohistory.org.

SECTION 7: OUR LOGO

LOGO COLORS

PMS 186C
C 12 M 99 Y 88 K 2
R 209 G 36 B 51
d12433

PMS 541C
C 100 M 76 Y 36 K 22
R 9 G 66 B 104
094268

LOGO HIERARCHY

When the Ohio History Connection logo appears in conjunction with other logos, the Ohio History Connection logo should be listed first. This applies to all Ohio History Connection materials.

ALTERNATIVE LOGO

When the logo appears smaller than .65 inches wide, the text-only option may be used. White space must still be maintained (see p 38).

SITE-SPECIFIC LOGO

Site-specific logos should be used on site websites and printed materials.

To request the official logo with a specific site name, contact Mallory Skrobot at mskrobot@ohiohistory.org.

 Armstrong Air & Space Museum

Figure 5.34, 5.35, 5.36, and 5.37. The Ohio History Connection's forty-page brand book lays out exactly how to use the logo, individually and in co-branding situations, plus acceptable color palettes. Ohio History Connection.

A. Spacing and Size

The Ohio History Connection logo rarely lives independently, therefore It is important to be mindful of other elements surrounding the logo. The logo should always remain proportionate to the artwork and never be illegible.

MINIMUM SPACE AROUND LOGO

All text and graphics should maintain a distance equal to the x-height of the "O" in Ohio from the logo. This also includes the edge of the art surface.

LOGO MINIMUM SIZE

For legibility, the logo should not appear smaller than .65 inches wide. For logo use smaller than .65 wide, use the alternative logo option provided (see p 37).

.65 in

SITE-SPECIFIC LOGO MINIMUM SIZE

For legibility, "Ohio History Connection" should not appear smaller than .65 inches wide. If the site specific logo does not fit within the given space, use the standard Ohio History Connection logo or approved alternative Ohio History Connection logo.

.65 in

Armstrong Air & Space Museum

SECTION 8

Our Look

A. Color Palette

The Ohio History Connection color palette is used to create a fun, curious, engaging tone. The goal is to create a visual look and feel that is bright, light and refreshing.

COLOR PROPORTIONS

- White should be the dominant value
- Accent palette should be used purposefully
- Gray should be used as a neutral to help colors and other elements stand out as needed

USE OF RED

Red is NOT included in the palette and should only be used in the logo.

PRIMARY PALETTE

LIGHT BLUE	MEDIUM BLUE	DARK BLUE
C 75 M 25 Y 5 K 0	C 85 M 40 Y 20 K 16	C 100 M 76 Y 36 K 22
R 38 G 154 B 205	R 16 G 112 B 148	R 9 G 66 B 104
# 269acd	# 107094	# 094268

NEUTRAL

GRAY
C 0 M 0 Y 0 K 25
R 199 G 200 B 202
c7c8ca

ACCENT PALETTE

PURPLE	YELLOW	ORANGE	GREEN
C 37 M 100 Y 20 K 0	C 0 M 22 Y 80 K 0	C 0 M 68 Y 79 K 0	C 40 M 0 Y 100 K 0
R 170 G 35 B 122	R 225 G 201 B 78	R 243 G 116 B 69	R 166 G 206 B 57
# aa237a	# e1c94e	# f37445	# a6ce39

SECTION 3

Our Personality and Voice

Often, voice is best defined this way: *If Ohio History Connection were a person, who would we be?*

Think of us as the History or Social Studies teacher students never forget. The one who helps them experience the past as something living and breathing. Her enthusiasm is infectious, yet completely down-to-earth.

A natural storyteller, she has a gift for helping others see events through her eyes and—through that act—understand how we are all connected. Though highly qualified to speak about history, she has a knack for communicating directly on your level. She doesn't put on airs or academic pretensions. Rather, her stories make you feel part of a larger, stimulating and relevant conversation.

That is the mission of the Ohio History Connection. We are the storytellers. And as others are drawn to the fire, they will find us there, ready to help them discover their connection to it all—often in ways they never expected.

Our Personality is that of the consummate storyteller—knowledgeable, approachable, passionate, fun, thought-provoking, dynamic and inclusive.

Our Voice is smart, friendly, vivid, specific and inspiring. Here's why:

- **Smart—**At the end of the day, we are the state's experts on Ohio's history. We should never forget our role as an authority that can bring knowledge to our communities.
- **Friendly—**We are not, however, intimidating. Our passion comes out as a sincere desire to engage with people. There are no bad questions. Our goal is to facilitate and make experiencing history easy.
- **Vivid—**While a certain topic may fascinate us personally, we'll lose our audience if we can't help them visualize it. A few colorful, well-placed words can bring our subjects to greater life.
- **Specific—**A "gleaming, bronze '57 Chevy Bel Air" is a lot more interesting than a "vintage car from the '50s." Generalities are dull; details conjure images. And reinforce our credibility as experts.
- **Inspiring—**Our job is to make history relevant for our customers. So the spark that makes an exhibit, site or event meaningful should shine through in our marketing copy.

Ohio History Connection • Brand Guidelines 8

SECTION 3: OUR PERSONALITY AND VOICE

VOICE: HIGH-LEVEL ADVICE

The following tips apply to high-level headlines, marketing teasers and event descriptions. You don't need to reinvent the wheel with your writing. But drawing on these dos and don'ts will help us keep our voice contemporary and on-brand.

DO:

Tell a story. People turn to the Ohio History Connection to discover the past—something that captures their imaginations, teaches them something new and even entertains them. Our sites and events may compete with a trip to the movies, COSI, television or a historical novel. So whether it's an exhibit teaser or a regional site description, our marketing copy should hook readers immediately.

DON'T:

Provide a dry report. This is the opportunity to show people that history doesn't have to feel dusty and bookish. Share your enthusiasm for the people and places you're writing about. Use specific details and vivid language. Or surprise your reader with a sense of humor. Our promise, after all, is to create memorable experiences.

EXAMPLE:

Before:

Rankin House

The Rankin House, located in Ripley, Ohio, was an important stop on the Underground Railroad, which provided safe houses for fugitives from slavery who were escaping to Canada.

After:

Rankin House

With its close proximity to the Ohio River and its owner's fierce opposition to slavery, the Rankin home made an ideal location for a safe house on the Underground Railroad. Learn how Rev. John Rankin and his family provided a "door of freedom" for more than 2,000 fugitives from slavery escaping to Canada.

Ohio History Connection • Brand Guidelines 9

Figure 5.38 and 5.39. The Ohio History Connection's brand voice book is a guide to writers developing anything from brochures to exhibit panels. Ohio History Connection.

SECTION 3: OUR PERSONALITY AND VOICE

DO:

Write for your audience. Our programs appeal to a wide array of audiences, ranging from general to specialist. Using specific call-outs or a shift in tone can target niche audiences, or conversely widen the group you're speaking to.

EXAMPLE:

Girl Scouts Are WAY More Than Cookies!

Discover two centuries of Girl Scout activities at this after-hours slumber party—and receive a special patch for attending!

DON'T:

Feel the need to use voice everywhere. Often, our guests simply need straightforward information without the presence of brand voice. Some texts require a more business-like tone, and others are more journalistic. Consider the context and audience, and judge for yourself what is most appropriate.

Ohio History Connection • Brand Guidelines 12

Figure 5.38 and 5.39. *(continued)*

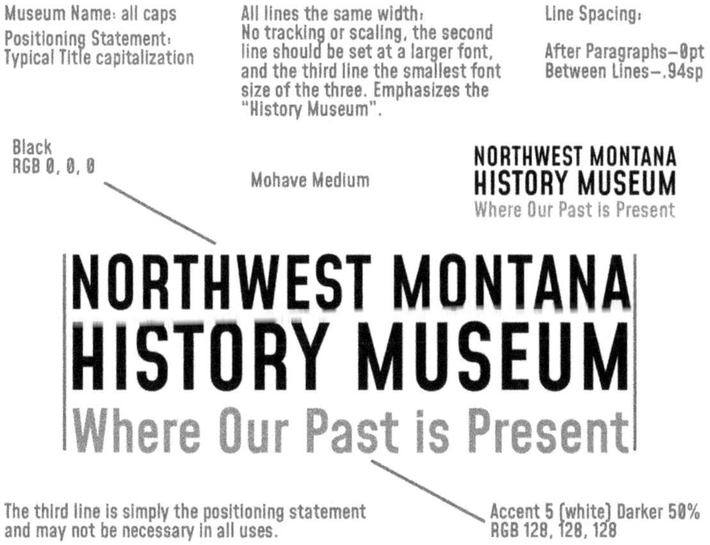

Museum Name: all caps
Positioning Statement: Typical Title capitalization
All lines the same width: No tracking or scaling, the second line should be set at a larger font, and the third line the smallest font size of the three. Emphasizes the "History Museum".
Line Spacing:
After Paragraphs—0pt
Between Lines—.94sp
Black
RGB 0, 0, 0
Mohave Medium
NORTHWEST MONTANA
HISTORY MUSEUM
Where Our Past is Present
NORTHWEST MONTANA
HISTORY MUSEUM
Where Our Past is Present
The third line is simply the positioning statement and may not be necessary in all uses.
Accent 5 (white) Darker 50%
RGB 128, 128, 128

Figure 5.40. Although much smaller than the Ohio Historic Connection's branding guides, the Northwest Montana History Museum's brand guide, created by students at Flathead Community College, provides the logos, fonts, and colors for the new logo. A longer document is summarized in this one-page "cheat sheet." Northwest Montana History Museum.

NOTES

1. Casie Vance (executive director) in discussion with the author, May 2020.

2. Shoshana Wasserman (deputy director) in discussion with the author, July 2020.

3. "Home," LaPlaca Cohen, accessed January 16, 2020, https://www.laplacacohen .com/.

4. Bill Chiaravalle, "Brand Navigation," accessed January 16, 2021, https:// brandnavigation.com/bio.

5. "About Us," First Americans Museum, accessed January 16, 2021, https:// famok.org/about-us/.

6. "Trademark Basics," United States Patent and Trademark Office, accessed January 15, 2021, https://www.uspto.gov/trademarks/basics.

7. Molly Alloy (co-director) in discussion with the author, May 2020.

8. Michele Reese Granger (marketing director) in discussion with the author, January 2021.

9. "Home Page," Renate, accessed March 15, 2021, https://www.projectrenate. com/.

10. "Moab Research Rebranding Questionnaire," internal document provided by Forrest Rodgers, March 2021.

11. Forrest Rodgers (interim executive director) in discussion with the author, July 2020.

12. Kathleen Powers (trustee) in discussion with the author, January 2021.

13. Jacob Thomas (executive director) in discussion with the author, May 2020.

14. "Heritage," Pendleton Woolen Mills, accessed January 17, 2021, https://www .pendleton-usa.com/pendleton-heritage.htmll.

15. "Glacier National Park Blanket," Pendleton Woolen Mills, accessed January 17, 2021, https://www.pendleton-usa.com/product/glacier-national-park-blanket/ 70275.html.

16. Jamison Pack (chief marketing officer) in discussion with the author, May 2020.

17. Larissa Vigue Picard (executive director) in discussion with the author, May 2020.

18. Donna Odom (executive director) in discussion with the author, May 2020.

19. Diane A. Rhodes, "Perris Railway Museum Rolls into Future with New Name, Logo," *The Press Enterprise*, April 7, 2019, accessed January 6, 2021, https://www .pe.com/2019/04/07/perris-railway-museum-rolls-into-future-with-new-name-logo.

20. Diane A. Rhodes, "Perris Railway Museum Rolls into Future with New Name, Logo," *The Press Enterprise*, April 7, 2019, accessed January 6, 2021, https://www .pe.com/2019/04/07/perris-railway-museum-rolls-into-future-with-new-name-logo.

21. James Harwell (creative director, Godwin Group) in an email to the author, January 2021.

22. Katie Blount (director, Mississippi Department of Archives and History) in discussion with the author, August 2020.

23. Pamela Junior (museum director) in discussion with the author, August 2020.

24. Cindy Gardner (museum division director) in discussion with the author, August 2020.

25. Jamie Bosket (chief executive officer) in discussion with the author, June 2020.

26. Judy Zulfiqar (chief strategist, Watermark Associates) in discussion with the author, August 2020.

CHAPTER 6

It's Time to Go Live

When the Montclair History Center was preparing to rebrand, board member and graphic designer Kathleen Powers laid out all its collateral material on a conference room table. Nothing matched. She then suggested they do the same thing with material from other organizations whose branding was cohesive. This simple exercise helped the team understand how a brand can morph across different media yet maintain a consistent look in print and online.

As you begin to think about rolling out your new brand, you need to balance your idea of an ideal launch with what you can afford and what your staff can manage. While you may want to usher in your rebrand all at once, it is often impossible given a limited budget and time. The good news is that even people who aimed for an all-in-one launch but got delayed for one reason or another said, in the end, it was all okay.

Most launches begin with a soft announcement to members, donors, and key individuals followed by a press release to area media outlets. Changing over the website and social media is often simultaneous or occurs shortly thereafter. Then comes the massive task of rebranding everything else from billboards to business cards.

In this chapter, we'll talk about each element of the launch, as well as timing, and share tips and lessons learned from people who have lived through it. After you read this chapter, you will be ready to create a launch plan that spells out *what* you need to rebrand and a timeline that outlines *when* you plan to do it.

A BIG REVEAL OR PHASED-IN APPROACH?

On December 13, 2019, Oklahoma City's News4 KFOR.com announced "the former American Indian Cultural Center and Museum will now be known as the First Americans Museum." The article quotes James Pepper Henry, First Americans Museum executive director, linking the rebranding to the museum's mission: "Our new name helps convey the institute's intention to share stories, history, and cultural lifeways past, present, and future."[1]

The media coverage was the result of a well-orchestrated press conference that featured the mayor, the chairman of the museum's board of trustees, and the executive director. It included a reveal of the name, a brand video that had been produced by the agency, and an update on the plans for the museum's opening. Prior to the press conference, the new name and look had been shrouded in secrecy. "We were basically able to flip a switch," says Shoshana Wasserman, who admits she was surprised they were able to pull it off.[2]

At the Virginia Museum of History and Culture, the launch was concentrated to one week. Every day over the span of that week, they sent emails or letters to different constituencies telling them about the upcoming change and building anticipation. At the end of that week, they uncovered the signs, rebranded the website, changed their email signatures, and began using new letterhead.[3]

Judy Zulfiqar, who often leads organizations through the rebranding process with her company Watermark Associates, says her team usually starts with a press release that introduces the new brand and logo. Simultaneously, they go live with the website. They develop a list of all the collateral material and assets that need to be rebranded, including business systems, promotional literature, and on-site and off-site signage. Their goal is to check off as many boxes as possible by launch.[4]

In reality, particularly at organizations with small budgets, a rollout happens over time. At most of the organizations featured in *Rebranding: A Guide for Historic Houses, Museums, Sites, and Organizations*, the process took three to six months from the day the new brand identity was introduced.

Many of the leaders at the thirteen sites had identified a go-live date that was either linked to a specific date or event or was chosen arbitrarily.

- Jacob Thomas says they launched the new Northwest Montana History Museum branding at an event they dubbed "Founder's Night," to honor those who saved the Central School from demolition and started the museum.[5]
- Donna Odom of the Society for History and Racial Equity (SHARE) says they created an event and invited other social justice organizations in town to launch the new dual mission, name, and logo.[6]

- Pejepscot History Center's reveal was designed to coincide with Maine's Bicentennial celebration.[7]
- The board of trustees at the Montclair History Center first revealed the new name and logo at an annual meeting in June, but randomly chose the following January to go live with a new website, signage, literature, and business material.
- Casie Vance at Ames History Museum says they were launching a capital campaign and wanted to have the new name in place prior to its kickoff. They announced the rebrand in a press release and on social media at the beginning of August. By early September, they had changed the website. "Everything else changed over slowly as we noticed it had the old name and logo on it," recalls Casie.[8]
- At Five Oaks Museum, "we were doing it all in-house, so we did it at a pace that was possible for us," says Molly Alloy. "It didn't just explode on January 1."[9]

If you decide to link your launch to a certain date, particularly one tied to a nonmoveable event like an anniversary or annual meeting, make sure you create a realistic timeline leading up to it that considers your staffing, budget, and the inevitable unforeseen circumstances.

As you create your timeline, identify if, how, and when each of the following components need to be part of your launch.

MEMBERS' ANNOUNCEMENT

You may want to tell members about your rebranding prior to the public announcement. This step can help members feel included in the inner circle and keep them from being blindsided when the announcement becomes public. Because they are also the ones most likely to have strong opinions about the change, it gives you an opportunity to address their concerns one-on-one, away from the general public. You may even develop a few advocates to support you when the rebranding goes live.

Depending on your timing, you can introduce them to your new brand at an event or meeting, in your newsletter, with an announcement letter, or via email. Whatever your vehicle, acknowledge the past positively, explain the rationale for the change, and make your case for why it is important to the future of your organization. The Montclair History Center's members received an insert in their newsletter after the name had been chosen but before the logo had been completed, as shown in figure 6.1. Titled "The Only Constant Is Change," it made the case for the new name.

A word of caution. The Ohio History Connection sent an announcement to their members prior to their press release. They didn't consider that

The One Constant in Life is Change...
Introducing the Montclair History Center.

We believe history is not just facts and figures. It's not just dates and battles. History is the stories of the people who have come before us and who, through their experiences, can guide us today. Our goal is to share those stories with you in ways that are unique, interesting, relevant, and fun.

To that end, consider attending a program on genealogy, architecture, military history, and women's history. Our Family FUNDays on the second Sunday of most months, gives parents and their children an opportunity to interact and discover history together. Join us on a walking, biking, and bus tour throughout Montclair.

If you haven't been to the Crane House in the last two years, please visit. We've reinterpreted it to convey a more complete history of Montclair, with two dedicated rooms, programs, and tours that tell the early 20th century story of the YWCA for African American women and girls. We also offer school programs that tell the story of the YWCA, Black history, de facto segregation, as well as the the early preservation movement in America. It also has a new name – The Crane House and Historic YWCA, reflecting its rich history.

Our Orange Road site now boasts a working microfarm made possible through a partnership with the Montclair Community Farm Coalition. Through the farm, we help people experience their agricultural roots by quite literally getting their hands dirty. The Landsberger Learning Garden, to be unveiled in the Spring 2017, will be a "please touch" garden where children and parents alike can discover the past and present uses of herbs.

Our library and archives have been expanded and organized, with searchable finding aids.

We've turned the museum shop into a Visitors' Center, where you can look at the 19th century general store and schoolroom and explore Montclair history as they wait for a tour. It also serves as charming classroom space.

We continue to look for new ways to best use the Shultz House, a remarkable, intact 19th century home located at 30 North Mountain Avenue.

Thanks to a bequest from the estate of Barbara Malcolm, a former member of the Board of Trustees and active participant at the Montclair Historical Society, we have established an Education Fund, which will be used to help schools that cannot afford to visit us.

We're also in the midst of developing a new website that will quickly and easily direct you to information about our programs, resources, or historic sites that may interest you, whether you're online at home or on your phone.

When our organization was founded 51 years ago, it consisted of one historic home. Today, we have four historic houses, a microfarm and learning garden, a library and archives. We are, in fact, a place to visit. A history center.

Our old name served us well for 50 years. As we look ahead to the next 50 years, we believe our new name – **the Montclair History Center** – encapsulates all we have become and will continue to evolve into. We hope you'll be part of our future.

The Montclair Historical Society receives an operating support grant from the New Jersey Historical Commission, a division of the Department of State. The Montclair Historical Society is a a501c3 organization. All donations are deductible to the fullest extent of the law.

Figure 6.1. The Montclair History Center created a document explaining the rebranding and sent it to its members. Montclair History Center.

several members worked in media. "One journalist scooped it and ran it as news," recalls Jamison Pack. "At the time, I was upset but in hindsight, I realize it was great. Someone saw it as newsworthy and covered it in a positive way."[10]

THE MEDIA

A press release is a standard way to let the world know about your new rebrand, plus you can frame the story. You can explain why you rebranded and what it means to your organization as *you* want it known to the public. The challenge, however, is that while rebranding has likely dominated your life for the last few months, it may be a nonevent to the media.

"There wasn't a big buzz in response to our press release," recalls Molly from Five Oaks Museum. They had issued a press release and unveiled the museum's new website on January 1, 2020. Despite the overall lackluster response to their press release, one media source wrote three in-depth articles about the museum during the first week. Molly admits they stumbled into that press coverage by giving the outlet advance notice and release rights. Once the media outlet had published their first article, the Five Oaks Museum team distributed the press release to other media outlets. "It gave them an investment in our launch," says Molly. "One of my big learnings is how important it is to cultivate the relationship with the press in advance."

The Ohio History Connection also had excellent editorial coverage when the new name launched in 2014. "Third party endorsement is key," Jamison says. "If people question your rebranding, it helps to have a third party talking about why it's a good decision."

Like Molly, Jamison believes cultivation is the key. "When the reporters were drinking up the history of our organization, it clicked for me. What they write about today becomes history tomorrow," she says, noting that reporters have a real interest in the past. "The cost of building relationships with them is time. It's something anyone can do."

Your press release should include both the old and new names, your reasons for making the change, a quote or two from people in your organization (e.g., board chairman, executive director, museum founder), a high-resolution copy of the new logo in color and grayscale, and a contact person they can call for more information. If you include an interesting photo of the museum or a new exhibit, the outlet has the option of either running your press release as an article or as a longer caption under the photo. You can also attach a fact sheet about the history of your organization, its mission, sites, membership, parent organization, etc. The First Americans Museum's press release is shown in figure 6.2.

FOR IMMEDIATE RELEASE

Media Contact:
Katy Gustafson, APR
katy@goodengroup.com
405.200.5631

First Americans Museum Enhances Brand to Illustrate Mission

American Indian Cultural Center and Museum will open in spring 2021 under new brand, FAM

OKLAHOMA CITY (Dec. 12, 2019) – The American Indian Cultural Center and Museum today announced a new name and brand for the center: First Americans Museum (FAM). The new name, selected in part for its historical accuracy, illustrates FAM's future-focused mission to serve as a dynamic center that promotes awareness and understanding of the cultural diversity, authentic history and contributions of the 39 First American Tribal Nations in Oklahoma today.

"As we approach the opening of this world-class museum, I was in full agreement with the leadership of the initiative that it was appropriate to move forward with a brand that truly reflects the story we're going to tell here," said Oklahoma City Mayor David Holt. "As a proud Osage and a proud mayor, I am thrilled to see this exciting project move forward as the First Americans Museum. FAM will be a unique, global destination where we celebrate our Native culture and the 39 tribal nations in Oklahoma today."

FAM is located in the heart of Oklahoma at the crossroads of four major interstates, positioning it as the gateway to First American Nations both east and west. The institution will appeal broadly to local, national and international audiences, offering vibrant experiences for all ages, families, and individuals who want to engage in shared American history.

"This cultural center and museum will serve as a dynamic venue where tribal voices celebrate Native American culture and contributions to our state," said Bill Anoatubby, Chickasaw Nation governor and chairman of the Native American Cultural and Educational Authority. "Tribes are an active and stabilizing force in Oklahoma with deep and permanent roots. Through this museum, we carry forward our stories and culture for the benefit of all Americans today and in the future."

659 American Indian Blvd.
Oklahoma City, OK 73129-6100
405.594.2100
info@FAMok.org
FAMok.org

Figure 6.2. The First American's Museums press release announced the new identity. First Americans Museum.

While there is no one reference that adequately addresses all the complexities of many diverse nations in one concise term, the FAM brand was created to convey the institution's intention to share stories, history and cultural lifeways from the first-person perspective to create a unique visitor experience.

"Our mission at FAM is to promote awareness of First American cultures, past and present. Our geographic placement and innovative vision will allow FAM to serve as a gateway to tribes both to the east and the west," said Gregg Wadley, chairman of the American Indian Cultural Center Foundation. "We look forward to celebrating the cultural diversity, authentic history and contributions of the 39 First American Tribal Nations right here in Oklahoma."

The FAM logo, comprised of bold typography, vibrant colors and triangle motifs, is an inclusive and modern expression of First Americans' arts and cultures. Its accompanying tagline, "One Place, Many Nations," represents the 39 tribal nations and their relationships to the First Americans Museum.

"We are taking a bold approach to explore and honor the rich cultures of Oklahoma's First Americans in one central location," James Pepper Henry, executive director of the First Americans Museum said. "The First Americans Museum will be unique in the way it will share the histories and rich cultures of our tribes – through an immersive experience of live programming, exhibitions, art, food, music and dance."

FAM will provide an array of engaging and vibrant experiences including the Tribal Nations Gallery, Smithsonian Gallery, FAMily Discovery Center, two theaters, dining, shopping, and a wide array of programs and events. For more information about the First Americans Museum, visit FAMok.org and follow FAM on social media at First Americans Museum (Facebook, YouTube) and @FAMokMuseum (Instagram, Twitter).

About First Americans Museum

The First Americans Museum will serve as a dynamic center promoting awareness and educating the broader public about the unique cultures, diversity, history, contributions and resilience of the First American Nations in Oklahoma today.

Click here to download a digital media kit with visuals

###

You most likely have a media list already. Your rebranding is a good opportunity to expand the list beyond local outlets to include history bloggers, listservs, individual journalists, history associations, and trade publications. Depending on your budget, you may want to hire a public relations team or freelancer to develop your press release, send it out to media outlets, and make follow-up phone calls to key places. You can also subscribe to a newswire service to disseminate your press release, but this option is costly and unless your rebranding has national or statewide appeal, may be overkill.

THE WEBSITE

Your press release worked. Someone reads about your organization in the local paper. Intrigued, she goes online to find out more, but instead of discovering the vibrant organization described in the article she just read, she finds your pre-rebranding, out-of-date website. You may have just lost a potential visitor or donor.

Whether you are designing a new website from scratch or just refreshing your existing website with a new logo and color palette, it should be ready when you go live with your new brand.

"The Montclair History Center's new website went hand-in-hand with our rebranding," recalls Elizabeth Hynes. The old website was cumbersome to work with and not mobile friendly. "We sorely needed a new website around the same time we were rebranding." The design firm introduced them to Squarespace, and staff developed the website, migrating some content from the old website and creating new content. "We wanted a content-rich website, where people could go to find out about our organization and our community's history," says Angelica Diggs, the museum's assistant director at the time of the launch.[11] "The greatest challenge was finding a way to organize all the information on the website, so it was easy to navigate." The staff finds they need to periodically reorganize as the website's content continues to deepen.

Donna Odom admits SHARE's website is also still a work in progress, but most of it had been developed by the time they sponsored the event announcing their new name. It reflects their dual mission of Black history and racial healing and houses some of their oral histories, but ultimately Donna would like it to be more interactive.

When the First Americans Museum name was announced, the team created a temporary website, explains Shoshana Wasserman. Because the museum was still closed, it served as a teaser for the museum, outlining what the museum is about and providing ways for people to donate and volunteer, as shown in figure 6.3.

Figure 6.3. A temporary website was set up to introduce the "FAM" branding and to entice donors and volunteers. First Americans Museum.

Other people updated their websites rather than create a new one when it was time to launch. "We had rebuilt our website a couple of years ago," says Casie. "We weren't going to do anything crazy. It's the same website with the new logo and color palette,"as shown in figure 6.4.

Others say their organizations didn't have the budget to redesign the website simultaneously. Larissa Vigue-Picard acknowledges that they needed a website, "but that wasn't in the budget. When we launched, we just changed the colors, font, and logo."

Figure 6.4. Repurposing the old website, the Ames History Museum incorporated the new color palette and curvilinear features. Ames History Museum.

Similarly, Jamie Bosket at the Virginia Museum of History and Culture says that at launch time, they couldn't afford to overhaul the website. They put a "new skin" on the old website, with plans to discard it and create a new website in line with the design principles of their new brand at a later date.

Rebranding your website goes beyond just putting your new logo on top. As several people mentioned, they used their new color palette and fonts. Even if you are putting a "new skin" on the old website, take some time to incorporate your brand personality, using the appropriate voice, images, and brand vocabulary. Michele Reese Granger notes that they try to use images of people as often as possible as part of their branding. Figure 6.5 shows an image introducing one of their exhibits on its website's home page.

Figure 6.5.   Part of HistoryMiami Museum's branding is the use of people in photography. HistoryMiami Museum.

Make sure your website is mobile-friendly so people who visit on their phones or tablets experience your brand in the same way laptop and desktop users do. For example, SHARE's website reads effectively on both a laptop and mobile device, as shown in figures 6.6 and 6.7. Your website should reflect your visitor experience.

As you go through your website adjusting things, look for subsites hidden within your site's architecture. For example, if someone wants to donate, register for a class, or explore your digital collections, a link might take them to your PayPal page, EventBrite, or a digital asset management system. Even if you can't include a customized logo, make sure your organization's name is correct.

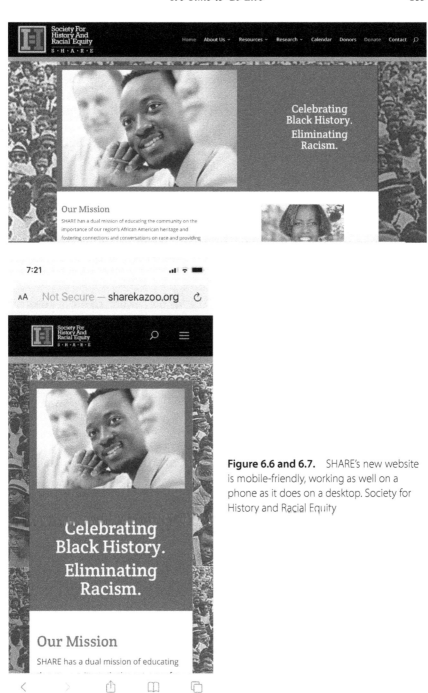

Figure 6.6 and 6.7. SHARE's new website is mobile-friendly, working as well on a phone as it does on a desktop. Society for History and Racial Equity

Finally, as you think about your website in relationship to your new brand, don't forget its URL. When Washington County Museum became Five Oaks Museum, the team wanted their URL to reflect the new name, so they bought the domain "fiveoaksmuseum.org." The Montclair History Center's old URL was "montclairhistorical.org," so they purchased "montclairhistory.org." SHARE now owns "sharekazoo.org," and Southern California Railway Museum is now "socalrailway.org." You can "point" your old URL to your new one so visitors to your old site will be redirected to the new site seamlessly.

SOCIAL MEDIA

Because social media is so ubiquitous, it's a great way to establish your brand with a broad audience. It's also relatively quick to do. The logo, images, posts, and voice on Facebook, Instagram, LinkedIn, and Twitter should all be consistent with your brand.

In some of the cases in *Rebranding: A Guide for Historic Houses, Museums, Sites, and Organizations*, social media was the first platform in the launch. When Pejepscot History Center's annual meeting was canceled because of COVID-19, they needed to find a way to launch the rebrand. Although they held an impromptu annual meeting online, that reached a limited number of people. They decided to announce it to the public on social media. Likewise, because Judy was running up against deadlines with Southern California Railway Museum's launch, "we started on social media, then moved to print ads. It was a progressive rollout over a period of time."

"The way most people have seen our new brand is through a social media rollout," explains Michele Reese Granger. "Social media is cost effective, and you can target the people who see it. I can spend a couple of hundred dollars on digital advertising and reach a huge audience. I couldn't do that with the *Miami Herald* or a billboard."

COMMUNICATIONS: PRINT AND DIGITAL

Think of all the ways you communicate with your audiences other than your website and social media: rack cards, brochures, newsletters, email newsletters, program announcements, fundraising letters, and more. Each of these need to be rebranded.

As you begin to rebrand this collateral material, keep in mind your brand is not simply a new name and look. All the organizations featured in *Rebranding* had undergone significant changes prior to or as part of their rebranding. Before you remove one logo and replace it with another, take an objective look at the copy and photos. If your goal is to attract families, but every photo in your brochure shows seniors in your museum, it's time for a photo shoot. If your goal is to appeal to a more diverse audience, but all your upcoming programs are about White founding fathers, it's time to expand your programming. If your goal is to project a friendly, less formal vibe, but your newsletter is written as if it's a peer-reviewed journal, it's time to edit. If your email blast has little to no branding, it's time to start designing.

As you begin rebranding print pieces, identify which are repeated often (e.g., a monthly rack card, a newsletter) and which are one-offs (e.g., a brochure that you reprint every year or two).

- Developing a template for often-repeated pieces helps you maintain a consistent look, plus it saves time and design costs. Depending on your in-house art talent, you could develop that template internally or ask the design team that created your logo, or because you have a brand guide, you can hand it off to someone who might be just as creative but less expensive. Once designed, staff can fill in the template as needed with the latest news or programs.
- For important one-off pieces, you may want to hire a writer and a designer to help. Since these pieces are redesigned less frequently and have a longer shelf life, it may be worth the additional cost to ensure you are getting something well written and well designed.

Online communications can be more challenging because you may be at the mercy of the design function built into your database management software. Many have templates you can adapt to echo your branding or have features that allow you to create one from scratch. An alternative is to design your online communications in another program, upload them as JPEGs or PDFs, and send them out to your email list.

"My hot tip is we use Canva," says Molly, referring to an online design website. "It suits us because we can be efficient and do it ourselves. If we have something special, we might hire someone to do it for us."

If you are interested in using a design website, there are others available in addition to Canva. Most of them have a monthly or annual fee but offer a free trial so you can decide which works best for you. Although Molly has an art background, these websites are created for the nondesigner and have well-designed templates you can use.

BUSINESS SYSTEMS

Letterhead. Envelopes. Business reply cards. Membership forms. Business cards. You can choose to have all these ready at launch or replace them over time as you run out.

Most of the people interviewed for *Rebranding* tried to complete their business systems by the go-live date. They recommend trying to use up old supplies when you know your go-live date is approaching. If you run out early, you can always create a temporary letterhead in-house by inserting your old logo into a document.

Although designing business forms is not overly creative, there are design choices you need to make. Where is the logo placed? Flush left? Centered? Flush right? Is it in color or black-and-white? Where is the address? Is it stacked or in one line? Do you list board members? What paper stock should you use? White, cream, or gray? Is your business card horizontal or vertical? One side or two?

If you regularly work with a graphic designer or have one in-house, he or she can help with these decisions. A local printing company may be able to send you several designs to choose from. Online print services (e.g., Vistaprint, GotPrint, Moo) are also good resources for creating business systems.

SIGNAGE

Casie Vance says the new exterior sign for the Ames History Museum was among the last items on their list to rebrand. Then, one day a visitor said, "I never noticed this building before, but I saw your sign. It looks different, so I came in." In hindsight, Casie says, "If we had known that would be the reaction, we might have done the sign earlier."

A common refrain is that exterior signage took longer and cost more than anyone had expected. Jacob Thomas said they removed the Museum at Central School sign when they launched the new name in September, but it took longer than anticipated to design, produce, and replace it with a new one.

Larissa Vigue Picard says they wanted to change the sign in front of the Pejepscot History Center, but because they were changing the wording and material, they needed town approval. Once they received town approval, there was another delay. "We're in Maine," she says. "If you are going to put signs in the ground, you have to wait until it thaws in the spring."

"Advertising" refers to the ads you pay for—from a $10 Facebook boost to a multimedia campaign. Your choices depend on your goals, location, and budget. Many of the smaller organizations in *Rebranding* didn't advertise at launch because of cost. However, if there's only one road that leads into town and you want to attract tourists, a billboard may be worth the expense.

Advertising options are evolving rapidly. Years ago, ad choices included newspapers, magazines, radio, television, and outdoor advertising (e.g., billboards, bus kiosks, subway ads). Today, you also have digital advertising where your ad will be seen by targeted audiences online through social media, Internet searches, and streaming applications.

Figure 6.8. When the Montclair History Center knew its signs wouldn't be ready by launch, they installed a temporary banner introducing the new branding. Montclair History Center.

If you are considering buying ads, understand what you are purchasing. Will your print ad also appear on the paper's website? Will it cost extra? What is the "reach?" How many "impressions" or "eyeballs" will see it? How often? Is there a mechanism to show you not just how people see or hear it, but how many people engage with it? Can you choose your audiences? Is production included? Ask lots of questions until you are confident the money you are spending will give you a strong return on investment.

As you move inside, think about exhibits as well as directional and informational signage. Generally, most people said they planned to update permanent exhibits as time and budget allowed. They didn't plan to update temporary exhibits but would incorporate the branding as new ones are developed.

Directional and informational signs should be refreshed to include the new logo, font, color palette, and tone of voice. For some organizations, this change happened immediately; others phased it in. Every sign at your site—from the welcome sign to the sign directing people to the restrooms— is part of the visitor experience. The more they reflect your brand, the more cohesive the experience.

EVERYTHING ELSE

You'd be surprised at what has your old name on it that you hadn't thought about. "Changing our name online—the yellow pages, museum associations, chamber of commerce, local visitors' bureaus—was a ton of work that I hadn't expected," recalls Jacob. Every time he thought he had completed the task, he would find another site with the old name. "There's no easy way to do it all at once," he says. "You have to go to each and every site and change it." In addition to the sites Jacob identified, your organization likely appears on Wikipedia, Google My Business, Yelp, Trip Advisor, LinkedIn, Indeed, and many other websites. These mentions are often overlooked until you stumble across them. One way to find them proactively is by typing your old name into a search engine and see what pops up.

Another often overlooked area is your gift shop. "Years after we rebranded, I was walking through the gift shop and saw greeting cards that said 'Ohio Historical Society,'" says Jamison. "Then there are notebooks, fleeces, T-shirts, and more. When we first rebranded, the staff intellectually knew we couldn't use them, but it felt like such a waste," she recalls. "Sometimes, we were downright sneaky getting rid of things." She recommends creating a plan for phasing out these items as launch nears.

Southern California Railway Museum relies heavily on its 1,500 volunteers to staff events and run, restore, and maintain the trains and trolleys. All volunteers have business cards, name tags, and branded shirts. As you consider what you need to rebrand, don't forget staff and volunteer identification.

"Look at how many pieces actually have your logo on it," advises Michele Reese Granger. "I underestimated the cost to truly rebrand because there are things that have your logo on it that you don't even remember—like the parking garage sign."

Finally, while this chapter addresses the most common media associated with a rollout, think creatively. Build a logo-themed float for the local Fourth of July parade. Hang a banner with your historic site's new branding on a railroad trestle. Even have it towed by an airplane. Sometimes, the sky is (literally) the limit.

NEXT STEPS

It's time to develop a launch plan with a timeline. Consider each of the elements outlined in this chapter and decide what you want to include in the rebrand. To make sure you haven't forgotten anything, wander around your site, creating a comprehensive list of everything you see that you'd like to brand. Some of these items may have your old branding, others may be as yet unbranded. Next, think about digital items. Website, social media, and digital collections first come to mind, but type your organization's name into a search engine and see else what comes up.

Once you know what will be included, decide on the flow of your rollout. As you create the timeline, begin with any hard dates—an annual meeting or an anniversary—that you want to use to launch your new brand. Then work backward, allowing plenty of time for design, production, and approvals.

In chapter 7, you'll begin to assign costs to all the elements of your launch plan.

ASK YOURSELF

1. Do you want to "flip a switch" and launch it all at once or do you want to phase it in as time and budget allows?
2. Is there a date or event you want to tie the launch too? An anniversary? Town-wide celebration? Upcoming campaign?
3. What is a realistic "go-live" target date, several months after your name can legally be used and your logo and brand guide will be complete? This date is when you distribute your press release, change over your website, and rebrand your social media platforms.
4. When do you want to inform your key donors, members, and other constituents?
5. What collateral pieces do you need to rebrand? Be specific. Identify every sign, each element of the business system, and every promotional piece. Set a target completion date for each of these items, keeping in mind whether you will do them in-house, hire someone to help, and your budget.
6. Your timeline now has your target dates to complete every item you need to rebrand. Working backward, how long will it take to complete each one? Break down the timeline into development (i.e., writing and design), internal and external approvals, revisions, final sign-off, and production.
7. Are there items you need to phase out? What, for example, is the last date you will reorder your old letterhead, volunteer T-shirts, mugs, brochures, to ensure you are not throwing a lot out once you go live? Note these dates on your timeline too.
8. Share your timeline with others to make sure you are being realistic and not missing anything.

NOTES

1. "First Americans Museum: OKC Native American Museum Announces New Name," KFOR.com, accessed January 20, 2021, https://kfor.com/news/first-ameri cans-museum-okc-native-american-museum-announces-new-name/.

2. Shoshana Wasserman (deputy director) in discussion with the author, July 2020.

3. Jamie Bosket (chief executive officer) in discussion with the author, June 2020.

4. Judy Zulfiqar (chief strategist, Watermark Associates) in discussion with the author, August 2020.

5. Jacob Thomas (executive director) in discussion with the author, May 2020.

6. Donna Odom (executive director) in discussion with the author, May 2020.

7. Larissa Vigue Picard (executive director, Pejepscot History Center) in discussion with the author, May 2020.

8. Casie Vance (executive director) in discussion with the author, May 2020.

9. Molly Alloy (co-director) in discussion with the author, May 2020.

10. Jamison Pack (chief marketing officer) in discussion with the author, May 2020.

11. Angelica Diggs (former assistant director) in discussion with the author, September 2020.

12. Michele Reese Granger (marketing director) in discussion with the author, January 2021.

CHAPTER 7

How Much Will It Cost?

The organizations featured in *Rebranding: A Guide for Historic Houses, Museums, Sites, and Organizations* spent drastically different amounts to rebrand—from $2,750 to over $350,000. These differences were seen across the board, in the research, design, and rollout phases. Even fees for filing for a name change varied greatly from state to state.

Your costs will depend on where your organization is located, whether you are using in-house talent or need to outsource it, and if you are outsourcing to an individual or a large agency. Your costs are also dependent on the extent of the rebranding. Are you updating your website or starting new? How big is your museum site and how many signs do you need to produce? How many collateral pieces are you rebranding and printing? How extensively do you plan to advertise?

This chapter is set up differently from others in *Rebranding*. It includes an outline to help you develop a budget for the launch plan. The outline includes both obvious and hidden costs, drawn from your colleagues' experiences. Because it includes all the research possibilities discussed in chapter 3, legal routes in chapter 4, design options in chapter 5, and rollout tactics in chapter 6, you may see something that doesn't apply to your organization. Cross it off and move on. To create an accurate budget for your location and situation, ask vendors for price quotes, speak with colleagues, or issue a request for proposal.

As you develop your budget, keep in mind there are always trade-offs. Although your costs will be lower if you choose to do most of the rollout internally, it will shift staff from their regular, mission-driven work to the rebranding effort and may require you to pay overtime. If you choose to extend the rollout over many months to spread out the expenses, it may take longer for the public to get used to your new name.

Once you have figured out what it costs, you can begin to figure how you will pay for it. At the end of the chapter, your colleagues share how they funded their organization's rebranding efforts.

Sharpen your pencil or open a spreadsheet. With the launch plan in hand and this outline, you can begin to create a budget for your organization's rebranding.

RESEARCH

Except for focus groups, which are most effectively done by a research company, each tool below can be scaled up or down depending on your time and your budget. For example, if you conduct a community gathering on-site, invite people via email, have someone internal serve as moderator, serve coffee and a simple continental breakfast, and produce the meeting materials in-house, you can likely keep your costs per meeting under $250 per event plus staff costs. On the other end of the spectrum, if you hire a consultant, send printed invitations, hold the meeting off-site with a full catered lunch, and create high-end meeting materials, your costs can skyrocket. The outline below will help you think through your options. Refer to chapter 3 for additional information about these research tools.

Focus Groups

A tried-and-true approach to market research, focus groups are one of the more expensive options to get qualitative research, unless you can find an organization that will donate its services. Potential costs include:

- Market research firm to design and conduct the focus groups
- Compensation for focus group participants
- Development of presentation material (e.g., large boards with logo options)
- Other?

Community Gatherings

Also known as "charettes," community gatherings can be inexpensive and are a great way to get the community invested in your rebranding efforts. Potential costs include:

- Consultant/moderator to help design community gathering(s), invite participants, lead, and develop summary report if you are not using someone in-house

- Design, printing, and mailing of invitations, unless you are relying on digital invites only
- Meeting materials
- Site rental costs
- Refreshments
- Small thank you gifts/"swag" bags
- Web-conferencing fees if you plan to conduct the gathering online
- Other?

One-on-One Interviews

Unlike focus groups or community gatherings, where the conversation may be swayed by one or two people with strong opinions, one-on-one interviews give you pure responses. Done internally, they are inexpensive and can yield solid information. They are, however, time consuming. Potential costs include:

- Interviewer if you are not conducting internally
- Web-conferencing fees if you plan to conduct the interviews online
- Other?

Surveys

With so many survey tools available online, conducting a survey is simple. Costs add up when you begin to use paid features or conduct in-person surveys. Potential costs include:

- Market research firm to design, field, and interpret the survey
- Paid features for an online survey
- Paying for additional, randomized responses through survey provider
- Tablet for in-person survey response collection
- Other?

Polls

A one- or two-question poll can be a cost-effective way to get a feel for public opinion, particularly if you conduct the poll at one of your own events or programs. Potential costs include:

- Exhibitor fee if you are conducting the poll at a fair or show
- Mechanism for conducting poll (e.g., cans, small objects, word cards)
- Small incentives for participation
- Consultant fee if you are hiring someone to conduct and/or staff it
- Other?

LEGAL NAME CHANGE

Changing a name is not expensive. Costs increase if you choose to hire a professional to lead you through the process. As you plan your upcoming budgets, remember that in some states DBAs require periodic renewals, although the fees are usually nominal. Refer to chapter 4 for additional information about the two paths you can take to change the organization's name. Potential costs include:

- Consulting fees for attorney or accountant
- Application and/or filing fees
- Other?

THE DESIGN PROCESS

The design process and the rollout will be the two largest chunks in your budget. Generally, an independent graphic designer will be less costly than a larger agency, but the agency may have more rebranding expertise. Whichever route you choose, find a designer or team that understands you, your organization's past, and its goals for the future. Refer to chapter 5 for additional information about the design process.

Brand Design

This includes everything from the initial input to the delivery of a brand guide. You may be given a quote on an hourly rate or on a project basis. Potential costs include:

- Outside agency or consultant to create the brand strategy, present design options, refine the design, provide camera-ready artwork and a brand guide
- Development of presentation materials (e.g., for board presentation and approval)
- Additional research to test designs (e.g., focus groups, polls)
- Other?

Licensing/Trademarking

If you choose to trademark the organization's new name or logo and/or license a font, potential costs include:

- Attorney with a specialty in trademarks
- Trademark application fee

- Purchase or licensing of font
- Other?

THE ROLLOUT

There are tremendous variations in rollout costs, based on how you plan to roll out the launch, the media you use, the size of your historic site, and the number of people you want to reach. The following list serves as a menu for all the options listed in chapter 6. Refer to that chapter for additional information.

Launch Event

If you plan to have a launch event, the key variables are location, size of the guest list if you plan to serve food, and how you plan to introduce the new brand. An off-site event with 350 guests, a sit-down dinner, and a pre-produced video is at one end of the spectrum. A wine-and-cheese gathering with fifty people at your historic site with boards introducing the new look is at the other. Potential costs include:

- Design, printing, and mailing invitations unless you are relying on digital invites only
- Site rental fees if not on-site
- Launch materials (e.g., PowerPoint presentation, preproduced video)
- Event planner
- Miscellaneous (e.g., programs, branded napkins, and cups)
- Refreshments
- Giveaways
- Additional staffing
- Other?

Members' Announcement

Costs depend on the size of your membership and whether you are introducing it via a printed mailing or digital. If you are sending it through regular mail, you may also want to consider including a branded promotional item, such as a magnet or tote bag. Potential costs include:

- Design, printing, and mailing announcement unless you are relying on digital announcements only
- Promotional item
- Other?

Media Announcement

Unless you plan to hire a public relations consultant, the media announcement is usually done in-house at little cost. Potential costs include:

- Public relations firm or consultant
- Newswire service fees
- Other?

Press Conference

Small organizations generally do not need to include a press conference in their budget. A few well-placed phone calls can work just as effectively for a lower cost. If you do plan to host a press conference, potential costs include:

- Launch materials (e.g., presentations, videos, display boards)
- Press kit
- Refreshments
- Site rental costs if not on-site
- Other?

Website

As you develop a budget for a website, your first decision is whether you plan to create a completely new website or update your existing one. Remember to think about all components of your website—font, logo, photography, programming, tone of voice, etc. Potential costs include:

- Website designer
- Writer to develop copy for the website
- Photographer
- Hosting contract with website builder (e.g., WordPress, Squarespace)
- Purchase of domain name
- Employee training on how to update the website
- Other?

Social Media

This line item refers to the unpaid use of social media, not advertising. In general, these costs are low unless you plan to hire someone to oversee your social media accounts. Potential costs include:

- Consultant to oversee social media accounts
- Other?

Print/Online Communications

As you develop this budget, think about which items you want ready at launch. It may be everything or you may choose to phase certain items in over time. Potential costs include:

- Graphic designer and/or writer to develop brochures, rack cards, post-cards, exhibit booklets, newsletter, and all other print material
- Graphic designer to develop templates for commonly used print and online items (e.g., newsletters, upcoming events)
- Photographer
- Print costs
- Fees associated with design websites (e.g., Canva) if you are designing internally
- Other?

Business Systems

A straightforward budget item. Several people said they included it as part of their general operating budget instead of the rebranding budget. Potential costs include:

- Graphic designer for letterhead, envelopes, business reply envelopes, business cards, membership forms, and name tags
- Printing all the above
- Other?

Signage

Consider all signage—on- and off-site—that needs to be updated or re-placed. Potential costs include:

- Design, fabrication, and installation of all exterior signage (e.g., building signs, banners, parking lot, directional signage, informational signage)
- Design, fabrication, and installation of interior educational and directional signage
- Design, fabrication, fees, and installation of directional signs not located on-site (e.g., state historic site markers, highway signs)
- Other?

Advertising

This line item includes all advertising, from inexpensive social media ads to billboards. Make sure you budget for ad design or development, placement, and in some cases, installation. Depending on your advertising plan, potential costs include:

- Design and ad space costs for ads in newspapers, magazines, and travel directories
- Development and cost of television and/or radio ads
- Design, fabrication, and installation of outdoor advertising such as billboards, bus and subway signs, kiosks
- Design and placement of social media digital ads
- Marketing consultant to oversee advertising associated with launch
- Other?

Branded Promotional Items

When the new logo is ready, it's tempting to put it everywhere. You want to make sure the gift store is stocked, you have apparel for staff and volunteers (if they wear it), and perhaps a couple of fun items to give to members. Although these items can be phased in over time, potential costs include:

- Apparel (e.g., hats, T-shirts, sweatshirts, tote bags)
- Gift items (e.g., mugs, glassware, coasters, ornaments, toys)
- Printed items (e.g., books, postcards, notecards, posters, magnets)
- Other?

FINDING THE FUNDS

Two organizations were fortunate enough to have single donors contribute a good part, if not all, of the funds needed to rebrand. At the Moab Museum, a generous donor funded the strategic planning and rebranding efforts. Forrest Rogers estimates the cost for rebranding alone was approximately $50,000.[1] Five Oaks Museum also received a generous donation from an individual that covered the website creation and development of the logo.[2] Not all organizations are that lucky.

Larissa Vigue Picard says most of the roughly $10,000 the Pejepscot History Center spent on the rebrand, from design to installation of exterior signage, was paid for out of the general operating budget.[3] The same was true for Southern California Railway Museum's rebranding.[4]

Several organizations found creative ways to underwrite or offset the costs of rebranding. At Northwest Montana History Center, Jacob Thomas found a pro bono website designer and developed the new logo at no cost through the local college. Each board trustee chipped in $100, offsetting the total expenditure of $4,000. He did not include reprinting business systems in his rebranding budget, rationalizing it as an expense he would have incurred without rebranding.[5] A market research firm donated its services to the Ohio History Connection, allowing them to field focus groups across the state at no cost.[6]

Having lived through an underfunded brand introduction in 2010, Jorge Zamanillo at HistoryMiami Museum chose to refresh the brand internally so they could allocate more funds to the rollout. Even with careful advanced planning, they underestimated the total cost of the rebranding rollout.[7]

After the Five Oaks Museum brand had been established, the team agreed they had the skill set to design their own collateral material in-house, saving graphic design fees. They also made the decision to concentrate their marketing efforts on the people who already knew them. "If we marketed to a wider sphere, we would be introducing ourselves to new people," says Molly Alloy. "Instead of spending that money, we believed we could reach the people who needed to know about the change through our newsletter and local paper. Others could find out about us over time."

Virginia Museum of History and Culture was on the other end of the spectrum. "From day one, we worked hard to increase our marketing spend and our willingness to actively promote the museum," says Jamie Bosket. He estimates they spent $50,000 on research and design and an additional $100,000 on the rollout.[8]

Local foundations may also be a source of support. Donna Odom received a grant from the Kalamazoo Community Foundation to pay for new branding for the Society for History and Racial Equity.[9] The Montclair Foundation helped offset costs for the Montclair History Center rebrand.

ASK YOURSELF

1. Is there an individual donor who might be willing to finance the rebranding either wholly or in part?
2. What foundations or corporations might be willing to support it? If either were credited on the home page of your website, signage, or brochures, would they be willing to underwrite the costs of developing it?
3. Would the board of trustees be open to making an in-kind or financial donation to support the rebranding?
4. Does the county or state offer grants for tourism projects?

5. Does your municipality offer grants for small businesses and nonprofits?
6. Could local high schools, vocational schools, universities be a source of interns or pro bono work?
7. Can online networks of pro bono consultants (e.g., TapRoot, Catchafire) provide any resources?
8. Are there any local market research companies or advertising agencies that might be willing to work for reduced fees or pro bono?
9. Does your bank (or the bank foundation) offer grants?

With your launch plan, timeline, and budget in place, you're prepared and ready to begin. Don't be surprised if someone says you're making a mistake or spending too much money. In chapter 8, your colleagues share how they managed the naysayers.

NOTES

1. Forrest Rogers (interim executive director) in discussion with the author, July 2020.
2. Molly Alloy (co-director) in discussion with the author, May 2020.
3. Larissa Vigue Picard (executive director) in discussion with the author, May 2020.
4. Judy Zulfiqar (chief strategist, Watermark Associates) in discussion with the author, August 2020.
5. Jacob Thomas (executive director) in discussion with the author, May 2020.
6. Jamison Pack (chief marketing officer) in discussion with the author, May 2020.
7. Jorge Zamanillo (executive director) in discussion with the author, July 2020.
8. Jamie Bosket (chief executive officer) in discussion with the author, June 2020.
9. Donna Odom (executive director) in discussion with the author, May 2020.

CHAPTER 8

The Naysayers

"When you are ready to change your name back, that's when we'll rejoin." Jamie Bosket remembers receiving membership renewals with this sentiment scrawled on the form. He says the Virginia Museum of History and Culture lost a few members when the museum began reaching beyond its members to offer public lectures and scholarships and again when the rebrand launched.[1]

Although he explained to naysayers the changes were additive and did not subtract from the work the Virginia Historical Society had always done, a few people refused to accept it. "We did lose members and we knew that would probably occur," he recalls. "We worked hard to mitigate that, but it inevitably did happen."

Jamie was not alone. Jacob Thomas, at the Northwest Montana History Museum, received an email telling him that renaming the museum was a "bad move."[2] Casie Vance recalls that people told her they didn't like the Ames History Museum's new logo.[3] Jamison Pack is confident people chose not to renew their Ohio History Connection membership. On a positive note, she says, "we only received a handful of negative responses. Less than ten."[4]

In this chapter, you will learn about some of the negative responses your colleagues encountered, what they may really be about, how they fielded them, and in some cases, even turned opinions around.

UNDERSTANDING THE NEGATIVITY

Many of the organizations featured in *Rebranding: A Guide for Historic Houses, Museums, Sites, and Organizations*, particularly those with a long history, experienced some level of public dissatisfaction with their rebranding.

When people say, "I don't like it" and "bad move," they are often not telling you the real reasons they are unhappy with the change. It's not always easy to tease out why someone is being negative. As Larissa Vigue Picard says, "when a person is horrified by your new name or logo, think of where the response is coming from."

The criticisms shared by their colleagues generally fell within three categories: the organization's mission or philosophy were evolving in ways the person didn't agree with or couldn't control, there have been too many changes, and the legacy that has endeared them to the organization is being lost.

An Evolving Organization

It's a commonly held belief people don't like change. Organizational psychologist Justin M. Deonarine, however, disputes that generalized idea. In an article in *Inc.*, he writes people accept change they can control, such as a change of scenery or a home remodeling. They don't like change that is forced on them, particularly if that change is intangible, like a new culture or values.[5] A rebrand, particularly if it signals a realignment in the organization's approach to history, is something out of the public's control.

"We have people who have been members for five decades and are remarkably dedicated," says Jamie. "If you have an affinity for an organization and have understood its identity for many years, you develop a great love and ownership of that organization. There is a certain degree of sensitivity to change," says Jamie. It's not surprising, therefore, when a person reacts negatively to something as intrinsic as the organization's name and identity.

As you saw in chapter 1, most of the organizations in *Rebranding* had indeed changed at their core, often by broadening the stories they tell and adopting a more inclusive stance. For some naysayers, the real issue is how the organization has evolved, not the rebrand. The rebrand, new name, or new logo is a smoke screen, an easy target. Chances are, nothing you say will change their minds.

Organizations whose names barely changed as part of the rebrand met with less negativity than more striking name changes. The minor move from the Museum of Moab to the Moab Museum was well received. Forrest Rogers says there had been backlash a dozen years earlier when a major donor's name, Dan O'Laurie, was removed from the museum's name and came down from the building. This time people said, "it's your original name" and "it's simple."[6]

Similarly, Jorge Zamanillo received mainly praise when HistoryMiami added "Museum," tweaked the font, and adopted new logo colors. He routinely heard comments like "more dynamic, welcoming, easier to read, clean," especially from younger audiences. All negative comments centered around the color. Although his team had deliberately chosen turquoise and pink because it represented Miami, some people thought it was *too* Miami. The colors reminded them of the 1980s television series *Miami Vice* and the Miami Heat basketball team when they suited up in their pink and blue uniforms.[7]

A One-Two Punch

Just as Jamie found people reacted to the changes in the museum's offerings *plus* a rebranding, others noticed the "one-two punch." One change people could live with. Two changes went too far.

"In 2014, we reinterpreted one of our museums to include the stories of the African American women who lived, worked, and played there in the twentieth century. Two-and-a-half years later, we rebranded," says Elizabeth Hynes.[8] Some people saw the two changes as cumulative, evidence that the Montclair Historical Society was fundamentally different. Although most people were in favor of the change, some people, particularly old-timers, were not.

Shortly after the new name was announced, a member sent an angry email, demanding to be removed from the membership roster and the mailing list. He claimed the change was the "last straw." Translation: first a reinterpretation, then a new name. His criticism was a built-up response to the many changes happening at the Montclair History Center.

Jamison Pack explains the Ohio History Connection made a second change in 2018 that elicited greater criticism than the name change in 2014. It too went to the heart of the organization's identity. "We had a quarterly magazine that many people assumed was a peer-reviewed journal," explains Jamison. "It was not peer-reviewed, but it had that perception. It cost us a lot of money and we were not getting new subscribers. The model was broken. We knew we needed to do something, so we merged our newsletter with the journal, and it became a bimonthly magazine."

The new forty-eight-page magazine includes a feature story and information about events and activities at the network's historic sites. It's an engaging publication, written in an informal tone of voice with lots of pictures. "We heard, 'There goes history. You are going to the gutter. You are dumbing down history,'" recalls Jamison. The critics believed the change, perhaps coupled with the new name, signaled a fundamental—and not welcome—change to their beloved historical society.

Loss of Legacy

Unlike most of the other organizations, First Americans Museum had not yet opened when it rebranded, so it did not have a history and longtime members. "When we changed the name, people said, 'Thank you, we never could say it, we never could remember it, we never could get our arms around it,'" says Shoshana Wasserman. "We've had a really positive and tremendous response."[9]

For museums that have been around for a while, it's not that easy. Historical societies, history museums, and historic houses are, by their very nature, concerned about preserving history. By rebranding, people may conclude you are trading a respected legacy for a shiny, new image. You are erasing your organization's history. These ideas may be a concern behind the generic "I don't like it" comments.

Loss of a legacy was at the heart of an earnest, thoughtful email the Montclair History Center received after announcing its new name. The writer explained the Montclair Historical Society had a long legacy and it would be a shame to lose that. "After several polite emails, we agreed to disagree and he wished us the best," recalls Elizabeth Hynes. He remained a member, participated in an oral history project, and even donated a scrapbook about the history of his house to the collections.

About a year later, he attended an event for another organization and started chatting with a younger woman about the Montclair History Center. "I just joined," she told him enthusiastically. "I never would have joined the Montclair Historical Society!" Shortly after their encounter, he sent an email to the Montclair History Center, shared what she had said, admitted he'd been wrong, and concluded with "you can teach an old dog new tricks."

Additionally, when leadership is new and has not built a rapport with the larger constituency, people may believe the "newbies" don't value the legacy. Molly Alloy and Nathanael Andreini had not served as co-directors long when they started to make the changes. "It weighed on my heart that we were coming new to the organization and making so many changes," Molly says. "We didn't come in to disrespect the organization as it was. We wanted to be of service and bring people who shaped and contributed to the organization along with us." Like Jamie, they worked hard in advance of and after the launch to explain the rationale for the change to key constituencies. "We didn't lose or alienate a single one of our vocal opponents."[10]

The question is, how do you manage and mitigate the negative responses?

MANAGING CRITICISM

"We reached out to every single one, regardless of their membership level. We tried to respond and explain the logic," recalls Jamie at the Virginia Museum of History and Culture. "I said to them, 'You believe this place is a treasure and that its historical assets are important to history, why wouldn't you want more people to be able to experience it?' For some people, that flipped the light switch on, but not for all."

Molly says, "We always thanked them for their generosity in taking the time and energy to tell us what they think and care about what happens to the museum." Molly and Nathanael spoke with people individually and accepted invitations to speak at community and affinity groups to explain their vision of Five Oaks Museum's future. They even published some of the negative emails in the newsletter so people could see their voices were being heard. After speaking with Molly individually, one woman renewed her membership and invited Five Oaks to speak at a group she was involved with. She had become an advocate.

Reviewing the results of your research, sharing the new vision for the organization's future, and explaining why the rebranding is essential to that future may help. At the very least, it may make the naysayers less vocal. At best, they could become advocates.

Sometimes, social media criticism can be the harshest and hardest to manage. One negative comment can result in a barrage of posts or tweets slamming your organization for making a change. Social media strategists agree it's best to respond quickly, positively, and without letting your emotions slip in.[11,12] Explain your rationale for the change succinctly and suggest they contact you directly to discuss it further.

Judy Zulfiqar has a crisis communications strategy in place for all Watermark Associates' clients. "We thank them for sharing their opinions and encourage them to take it off-line. 'Give us a call if you have any questions or concerns.'" In the case of Southern California Railway Museum, no one ever did.[13]

Several leaders shared stories about how third parties helped sway the naysayers. Before the Ames History Museum rolled out its new logo, Casie Vance and several board members invited former staff to a meeting. "They were retirees, still active, volunteering and attending events," she says. "They were also really set in the Ames Historical Society way. We brought them in to talk about the new name and logo and see what they thought because they represented the kind of people we believed might be worried about the change."

She was correct. "They were resistant to the change, worried about people being confused, worried about losing our old identity," Casie recalls. After the meeting, one woman who was opposed to the change printed out the old and new logos and began showing it to her family and at meetings. "Overwhelmingly, people of all ages liked the new one better," Casie continues. "She came back to us a couple weeks later and told us their reactions had changed her mind. She confirmed this was the right way to go."

At the Northwest Montana History Museum, Jacob Thomas knew "there are people who are still completely committed to Central School," the original name of the building that houses the museum. Although their numbers are dwindling, these people either attended Central School prior to its closing in 1969 or when it was part of the Flathead Valley Community College. He wanted to show them he was honoring the legacy, even though the name was changing.

"To partially address that, we installed a new permanent exhibit in the central hall," explains Jacob. "It's all about the school's history, the historical society, and saving the building." It pays homage to the people who led the way and addresses the questions most frequently asked by visitors. "It's a 22,000-square-foot brick building. It's still the biggest building in town, and people are naturally curious about where it came from and how we still have it today."

The Montclair History Center also honored its founders as part of a permanent exhibition. "When we reinterpreted and when we changed the name, we were careful to honor the people who had come before us," says Elizabeth, whose grandmother was a docent at the museum thirty-five years ago. "We tried to communicate that we were building on that heritage, not erasing it."

As part of the reinterpretation, the founders of the Montclair Historical Society are recognized for their contributions in saving the house from demolition in 1965. "They may not have done preservation the way we would today, but they did what they believed was best in days before the National Historic Preservation Act was even passed," says Elizabeth.

The good news is, everyone agreed that the positive feedback far outweighed the negative responses. You just need to be ready for the small number you may receive. As you launch your rebrand, prepare for the naysayers by answering the following questions. If you receive only positive reactions, even better.

ASK YOURSELF

1. Who is most likely to object to the change? What are they really objecting to? A name change? A value change? A culture change? The passage of an era?
2. Has your organization made other changes that may compound the critical comments?
3. Is there anything you can do to win over potential critics before the launch? One-on-one meetings with museum founders, long-term members, board members? Small community groups? A few well-placed phone calls?
4. Are there respected third-party advocates among the constituencies you're most concerned about? Are they willing to speak on your behalf about the need to rebrand?

5. Do you want or need to honor the legacy of the museum? How? An article in a newsletter? A permanent exhibit? A special event?
6. What talking points will you use to respond to comments by the public? The press? On social media? You may want to develop a formal list you can refer to. A consistent message is key.
7. If there are critics, who will respond to them? The executive director, a board member, a member of the marketing team? Designating a single person or two is wise to ensure the right messaging is conveyed.
8. Will you encourage people to take the conversation off-line, and if so, do you want them to call? Send an email? Drop-in?

The thirteen organizations each had different budgets, geographic locations, motivations, key constituencies, and challenges. In chapter 9, your colleagues sum up their rebranding experiences, share success stories, and offer advice based on their own experiences.

NOTES

1. Jamie Bosket (chief executive officer) in discussion with the author, June 2020.

2. Jacob Thomas (executive director) in discussion with the author, May 2020.

3. Casie Vance (executive director) in discussion with the author, May 2020.

4. Jamison Pack (chief marketing officer) in discussion with the author, May 2020.

5. Justine Deonarine, "The Psychology of Leading Change (Versus Merely Managing It)," *Inc.*, June 25, 2019, accessed February 1, 2021, https://www.inc.com/entrepreneurs-organization/the-psychology-of-leading-change-versus-merely-managing-it.html.

6. Forrest Rogers (interim executive director) in discussion with the author, July 2020.

7. Jorge Zamanillo (executive director) in discussion with the author, July 2020.

8. Elizabeth P. Hynes (president, board of trustees) in discussion with the author, October 2020.

9. Shoshana Wasserman (deputy director) in discussion with the author, July 2020.

10. Molly Alloy (co-director) in discussion with the author, May 2020.

11. Ann Tran, "Handling Social Media Criticism," *Entrepreneur*, accessed February 1, 2021, https://www.entrepreneur.com/article/235456.

12. Chad Reid, "Seven Tips for Handling Social Media Criticism," Jotform, accessed February 1, 2021, https://www.jotform.com/blog/handling-social-media-criticism/.

13. Judy Zulfiqar (chief strategist, Watermark Associates) in discussion with the author, August 2020.

CHAPTER 9

Success

You have now walked through the rebranding process with thirteen history organizations from across the country. The reasons your colleagues cited for the rebranding varied, but all boiled down to a combination of three:

- First, they wanted the new brand to embody deep-rooted, fundamental changes that had taken or were taking place in the organization.
- Second, they wanted to correct inaccuracies in their previous brand.
- Third, they believed their old branding created barriers and the rebrand would improve public perception.

The organizations varied in size, scope, staffing, and budget, but the process was basically the same. Some people orchestrated the rebranding with little or no assistance, and others had a formal committee. Some organizations spent less than $5,000, and others spent over $100,000. Some conducted research, and others relied on intuition. Each organization followed the same series of steps—identifying the need, finding a new name, designing the logo, implementing the launch, and responding to the public. Finally, almost everyone had a least one naysayer who didn't like the change.

Rationale and process were not the only commonalities. The leader of each organization has deemed their efforts "successful." Measures of success varied from qualitative feedback from the public to quantitative data about visitors and increased social engagement.

This chapter will reprise the impetus behind each organization's change and share some of their successes. With their rebrand behind them, your colleagues share their advice as you embark on your organization's rebranding.

AMES HISTORY MUSEUM

Ames, Iowa

Ames History Museum, formerly Ames Historical Society, is in a college town people flock to when they retire. The organization had a strong older adult base, but they wanted to expand their demographics. They began to offer more children and family programs and were about to launch a capital campaign to create a more hands-on, interactive exhibit space. The leadership believed "historical society" was a barrier and even the logo, says Casie Vance, "looked historical." Before they launched the capital campaign, the board decided to rebrand, accomplishing it in a record-fast five months— from decision, to rebrand, to the final elements of the rollout.

Casie says, like most of the organizations in *Rebranding: A Guide for Historic Houses, Museums, Sites, and Organizations*, they did not use research tools to evaluate whether the rebranding was a success. In hindsight, she says, "If we had planned better, we might have done more of this at the same time, but the way it worked out was fine." She says initially there was some confusion, and people are still writing checks to the Ames Historical Society, but "for the most part people have switched over."[1]

"I went into it thinking more people would be resistant to change, but we've barely gotten any negative comments," she says. Plus, with their new signage, they are now being noticed by people who pass by. The rebranding occurred quickly, without controversy, and has met with the public's approval.

Words of Wisdom

> "I went into this thinking more people would be resistant to change, but it went super smoothly."
>
> —Casie Vance

FIRST AMERICANS MUSEUM

Oklahoma City, Oklahoma

Before the museum doors opened, the American Indian Cultural Center and Museum's name changed to First Americans Museum. The former name was a mouthful, hard to remember, and inaccurately used the term "American Indian." In addition, because the project had been in development for decades, the leadership team wanted to "revitalize the organization, give it a sense of positivity, a sense of bold direction," recalls Shoshana Wasserman.[2]

"It was always our intention to be as inclusive as possible, but it really pushed us to think in those terms and make sure we were creating a brand that everybody could feel part of," says Shoshana. Initially, they accomplished this through informal focus groups with the key stakeholders and surveys. Once they were in the throes of developing their new name and look, they walked each of their board members individually through a presentation that explained the rationale for the change, why they had chosen the name "First Americans Museum," what the new logo looked like, and how it would be used. "We did some tweaking based on their questions and concerns. It was a really healthy process to get all of these different perspectives one-on-one, and as a result, we had tremendous buy-in."

Because the museum is not yet open, she can't rely on metrics, such as visitorship, that museums traditionally use. However, she says, "We've had a tremendous response from the public. Everyone who has commented says something like, 'Thank you. We could never say it, we could never remember it, we could never get our arms around it.'"

Words of Wisdom

> "Sometimes, you need somebody with a broader perspective to help balance the biases that you have locally. . . . It was always our intention to be as inclusive as possible, but it pushed us to think in those times and make sure that we were creating a brand that everybody could feel a part of."
>
> —Shoshana Wasserman

FIVE OAKS MUSEUM

Portland, Oregon

Five Oaks Museum had undergone a seismic change, and its leadership wanted the world to know it. They had revamped the organization's structure and adopted a set of values to guide them. Perhaps most dramatic, they changed the museum's entire approach to history, exposing the complex layers of history and giving voice to the communities' descendants. They also broadened how they tell their stories with art, music, and theater. The name "Five Oaks" is a metaphor for their layered approach to history. A nearby landmark, the five oaks had meaning for the indigenous people, traders, settlers, and farmers. By changing their name from the Washington County Museum, they publicly acknowledged the museum was about more than the Euro-American experience.

"The response has been dizzying," says Molly Alloy, noting they have gone from a museum no one had heard about to one receiving national recognition. "Our brand is not a marketing device. It is the spirit and personality of the organization we are building. People are moved that the organization is willing to peel back the onion and let there be a lot of layers to the stories we tell. The reality of this experience has surpassed my dreams. It feels not just like a retooling, but like a deep healing."[3]

"What we've learned in this process," Molly continues, "is that wherever we can tell what we did, instead of the idea we had, it moves our audiences, it moves our collaborators, it moves our funders, it moves our board. That's really the resounding positive response."

Words of Wisdom

"Use your heart. Mean what you say. Do what you say. Don't be afraid of doing it wrong. If it's sincere and transparent, you will find your way."

—Molly Alloy

HISTORYMIAMI MUSEUM

Miami, Florida

HistoryMiami Museum's rebranding was more of a tweak than a full rebrand. In 2010, the Historical Museum Southern Florida became HistoryMiami and adopted a bold, orange logo. According to Jorge Zamanillo, one of the biggest challenges was that no one knew what they were because the word "museum" wasn't in the name.[4] The color choice was limiting and wasn't readily associated with Miami. In addition, in the years since the 2010 rebrand, the organization had embraced the values of inclusion, diversity, equity, and access (IDEA), a movement aimed at minimizing bias and reducing systemic inequalities that put some individuals or groups at a disadvantage. After a decade, it was time to refresh the brand with accessibility in mind.

The brand refresh, as Jorge calls it, was handled internally as a collaborative process. Jorge believes strongly in the value of collaboration and letting voices be heard. However, while input is good, though, he cautions you need a leader who can say, "these are the parameters and here's who has the final decision." Without that leadership, you can wind up with a "mishmash of logos" no one is happy with.

The 2020 modifications included adding the word "museum" to the logo, changing the color palette, and adjusting the font. Their goal was to create a logo that people could identify as Miami and met all the criteria for ADA accessibility.

The launch coincided with COVID-19 shutdowns making it impossible to compare before and after metrics; however, the public response has been positive. Internally, the logo is a success. Because the staff was involved, they easily bought into the change. The logo meets all ADA guidelines regardless of which colors in the color palette the staff chooses and how the logo is used. It's easier to work with and more adaptable, and "museum" is now front and center in the organization's name.

Words of Wisdom

"Be collaborative, but make sure you have a leader."

—Jorge Zamanillo

MOAB MUSEUM

Moab, Utah

When Forrest arrived at the museum as a consultant, he asked the board, "What does your community want?" Did the community want a new state-of-the-art natural history and anthropology museum?

After conducting a community assessment, the board made the decision not to proceed with a $60 million capital campaign to build the Moab Museum of Natural and Cultural History. They instead agreed to proceed with a more modest overhaul of their existing space with fresh, new exhibits in a more museum-like space. With the input from the community, they refocused their exhibits on stories rather than objects.

Next, they needed a brand identity that communicated their changes to the local community as well as tourists passing through Moab on the way to the nearby national parks. They went back to their roots and chose "Moab Museum," a simple variation on the historical name, "Museum of Moab." They selected the tagline "Small Museum, Big Stories."

After they completed their renovation work at the museum, they were unable to reveal the new space or the new brand to the public with great fanfare because of COVID-19. That said, according to Forrest Rogers, the response to the new graphic identity has been positive from all audiences. Qualitative feedback will have to suffice for now. With a history of uneven record keeping in terms of attendance and membership, the Moab Museum is starting at baseline with their metrics.[5]

Words of Wisdom

"Be bold, but be informed by your community."

—Forrest Rogers

MONTCLAIR HISTORY CENTER

Montclair, New Jersey

The Montclair History Center had undergone a fundamental change by reinterpreting one of its historic house museums to include its history as a segregated YWCA for African American women and girls. As the organization expanded its programs, exhibits, and collections and confronted difficult subjects like Jim Crow in the North, telling more inclusive stories became part of the organization's DNA. The name change from the Montclair Historical Society to the Montclair History Center highlighted those fundamental changes to the public.

"We were convinced the term 'historical society' didn't convey the progressive things we were doing," says Elizabeth Hynes. "For the people who already knew us, it was okay. But our research showed us that it was keeping others away."[6]

It's impossible to determine whether the uptick in metrics can be attributed to a new name or the essential changes in the organization's overall brand. However, three years after the rebrand went live, the number of onsite visitors had increased by 59 percent, and website visits had increased by 53 percent. The Montclair History Center has seen similar growth in social media engagement and program attendance.

Success can be measured qualitatively too. As staff member Angelica Diggs says, "When your brand matches what you do, that's success."[7]

Words of Wisdom

"Don't let fear of the unknown or funding concerns stop you. You can always ask people for advice and find ways to make costs scalable so your organization can afford it."

—Elizabeth Hynes

"Begin with a design brief or brand strategy. It helps ensure the project stays on track."

—Kathleen Powers[8]

NORTHWEST MONTANA HISTORY MUSEUM

Kalispell, Montana

The name "Museum at Central School" was confusing. People didn't know if it was a school, a museum, or a museum about a school. As a result, although it is the largest building in town and on the direct path to Glacier Bay National Park and Preserve, tourists rarely stopped. "As you are rolling through Kalispell, you'd think it was a historic schoolhouse," says Jacob Thomas. "Our rebranding was very market conscious." Even a board member admitted the old name had never worked for them.[9]

Jacob Thomas oversaw a rebrand that led to a new, more self-explanatory name: Northwest Montana History Museum. Drawing on the talents of students at a local community college, Jacob and the board accomplished the rebrand smoothly and cost effectively—a must for an organization with an annual operating budget of less than $150,000.

The changeover occurred in the winter, always a slow time for the museum. And summer visitation was slowed by COVID-19, but Jacob says he's heard positive feedback from the community. "We've heard from many members and longtime supporters," says Jacob. "They have been completely positive about our changes."

Words of Wisdom

"It's rare in life to be able to be a full-out optimist. A rebranding allows you to do that. It allows you to think about what your museum can accomplish, and how if you change a couple of things, you can really fulfill your mission."

—Jacob Thomas

OHIO HISTORY CONNECTION

Columbus, Ohio

A question about membership led to a series of pro bono focus groups, which culminated in the agency telling the Ohio Historical Society's leadership that its name was a barrier to growth. The agency's assessment echoed years of membership and market data research.

The name also no longer accurately described the organization, which had evolved into the state's historic preservation office, state archives, local history office, museum and village, and an affiliate network of more than fifty sites throughout Ohio. Jamison describes another evolution. "We had been a collecting institution, and our priority was our collection. Today, our values are centered around serving the public, which includes understanding who they are and what they need in this moment."[10]

In 2013, the rebrand went live. The new Ohio History Connection brand—its name, logo, "voice," and interactions with the public—embody the shift from a collecting to a people-centric institution. Today, the new name and logo are firmly established in Columbus, where the organization is headquartered.

Although they have not tweaked the brand, they have tweaked their strategy. About three years after their new brand went live, they conducted a phone survey and found name recognition was low across the state. Jamison says, "I think, to really get that name recognition, our best efforts are working through our site partners and working throughout K–12 curriculum." Jamison is now working on co-branding its network of historical sites throughout Ohio.

Words of Wisdom

"Take advantage of digital advertising and social media to increase your organization's visibility. If you have limited ad dollars, spend them on digital advertising impressions. If you have a big event you want to promote or a unique story to tell, engage a social influencer with a large social media following and have them tell your story."

—Jamison Pack

PEJEPSCOT HISTORY CENTER

Pejepscot, Maine

As part of a strategic planning process, the Pejepscot Historical Society Board considered the organization's brand. They agreed to drop "historical society," believing it was an impediment to the public. Furthermore, they wanted their logo to broadly encompass the region's history rather than an architectural detail on one of the buildings. Their new name and abstract logo denoting the flow of a river does just that.

Larissa Vigue Picard admits at times the rebranding process was slow and frustrating. Although Larissa was working with a committee, she needed to stay closely involved, moving the process forward. "Make a realistic timeline and stick with it as closely as possible," she says.[11]

Larissa had not planned to conduct any post-rebrand surveys. She planned to rely on visitor metrics, particularly around audience demographics, to evaluate the combined effects of reinvigorated programming and the rebrand. A year after the rebrand, the museum was still not fully open due to COVID-19, putting that evaluation on hold.

Despite the shutdown, with the new name, logo, and programming, the public is taking notice of the Pejepscot History Center. "I meet people who say, 'For years you didn't hear anything about that place,'" says Larissa. "'There's a lot of energy there lately. You are doing some cool things.'" Larissa believes that even before the rebrand, "there was a groundswell happening. The rebranding was just the latest. You can change a name and change a logo, but it's people realizing what you do is different, what you offer is different."

Words of Wisdom

"Keep a tight rein on the process and be willing to adapt if needed. A sense of humor is key."

—Larissa Vigue Picard

SOCIETY FOR HISTORY AND RACIAL EQUITY

Kalamazoo, Michigan

When the Southwest Michigan Black Heritage Society's mission expanded beyond preserving local African American history to include a social justice focus on race, its leadership knew it was also time to change the name to reflect the new dual focus. They also wanted a catchy acronym. The Society for History and Racial Equity—or SHARE—met their goals.

Donna Odom went into the rebranding without even knowing what a rebranding was, learning as she went. For Donna, it was a satisfying endeavor. "We were so happy to be able to change our name," recalls Donna. "With that long name, nobody could ever remember it and there was no way to have an acronym."[12]

Name recognition happened fast. "I was so surprised to find out how quickly people started remembering it, knew who we were, and what we did," she recalls. "We do so much with that name now. Our newsletter is 'SHARE Out.' We did a cookbook called SHARE-ing Our Recipes." Like First Americans Museum's "FAM," the acronym opens endless possibilities for fundraising and marketing efforts.

Words of Wisdom

> "Funding is always a concern, but we were able to get more funding, better funding, once we expanded our mission and name."
>
> —Donna Odom

SOUTHERN CALIFORNIA RAILWAY MUSEUM

Perris, California

Southern California Railway Museum's former name, Orange Empire Railway Museum, was rooted in the organization's sixty-plus-year history, but in the twenty-first century, it caused confusion. Because the museum's audience now extends far beyond the region, the old name incorrectly led people to believe it was in nearby Orange County.

Leadership didn't have to venture far to find a new name. They had already legally changed the entity's name to Southern California Railway Museum but had never used it publicly, perhaps unwilling to give up the long legacy of the Orange Empire Railway Museum. The new logo's bright orange color pays homage to that legacy, giving a nod to the former name.[13]

When the name Southern California Railway Museum launched on the new website, positive comments such as "it's about time" and "this is great" spilled onto social media. With nearly 100 acres of property and outdoor advertising for miles around, the changeover has been a massive undertaking.[14] The board does not plan any follow-up research to determine the success of the new name.

Words of Wisdom

> "Focus on what your brand is, not whether the line is straight or curved or what the color is. Your brand is more than just a logo or name. It is how people feel about and/or experience your organization."
>
> —Judy Zulfiqar

TWO MISSISSIPPI MUSEUMS

Jackson, Mississippi

A year after the Mississippi Museum of History and the Mississippi Civil Rights Museum opened the doors, the leadership realized the two museums would benefit from combining their two staffs into one. They also realized it was important to stress to the public that the museums were independent yet worked synergistically to tell a complete story of Mississippi's history.

Even though this two-but-one concept had been incorporated into the logo from the beginning, they had not stressed it, concerned the public would be confused. Despite their concerns, the logo visually clarified the museums' relationship, and the public has adopted it wholeheartedly.

Pam Junior, who was selected to lead the unification of the two museums, says the Two Mississippi Museums "tell the community and people all over the world that these complex stories gel together. If you understand the stories, you understand Mississippi."[15]

The Two Mississippi Museums' staff is not planning on conducting research on name recognition, although Cindy Gardner admits that people routinely mix up the Museum of Mississippi History name, calling it the Mississippi History Museum, Mississippi Museum of History, or History Museum of Mississippi. "Back in 2002, we decided on the Museum of Mississippi History because we wanted to emphasize the connection to the Old Capital Museum of Mississippi History, which had been badly damaged by Hurricane Katrina," she says. She wonders if there might have been less confusion if the two museums' names echoed each other—Mississippi History Museum and Mississippi Civil Rights Museum.[16]

Katie Blount speaks of the combined museums' success in human terms. "A past governor came in numerous times to really understand civil rights here in Mississippi," she recalls. In the wake of the Black Lives Matter movement and the killing of George Floyd and other unarmed Black people, Katie says, "legislators wanted to come in with their families to tour the museums. I had some inspirational conversations about what they thought.

Not only did we change hearts and minds, but legislation is also being changed because they came into these museums."[17]

Words of Wisdom

"Think about how your name will be used and choose a name that the public will remember easily."

—Cindy Gardner

VIRGINIA MUSEUM OF HISTORY AND CULTURE

Richmond, Virginia

The rebranding of the Virginia Historical Society was part of a "massive and sweeping reorganization of the institution," says Jamie Bosket.[18] It included a period of introspection and reflection on what they wanted the organization to be and a comprehensive strategic planning process. During that process, research confirmed that "historical society" hindered public appeal. The leadership created a brand hierarchy, retaining the original name as the parent organization and changing the museum's name to the Virginia Museum of History and Culture.

"The public response was overwhelmingly positive," he says, but notes the response was due to far more than the launch of a new name and logo. The Virginia Museum of History and Culture had radically changed the museum, launching new programs, increasing outreach, and more proactively engaging the community. "We were not on the radar of a lot of people," says Jamie, but with all the changes there have been double-digit, and in some cases, triple-digit increases in foot traffic and social engagement.

"Historically, our attendance has followed a pretty similar trend to most traditional historical societies, but a major change happened, all directly related to our rebranding," explains Jamie. "2019 was our single busiest year ever in our history. We had about 110,000 people visit the museum, which is twice our historical average all the way up through until 2017. A rebranding is so much more than a name. Our branding was a reimagining of our organization."

Words of Wisdom

> "Understand where you want the organization to be several years down the road. Know what you want, what the community needs, and then back up and find out how the brand can articulate that."
>
> —Jamie Bosket

IT'S A WRAP

Regardless of how well you plan and how many people help, rebranding your organization is going to take a lot of time and energy. That's time and energy away from writing grants, meeting donors, strategic planning, program development, and the myriad other tasks associated with running a historic site or museum. As your colleagues can attest, rebranding is worth it if it:

- Better communicates what your organization is all about,
- Dispels old stereotypes,
- Attracts new audiences,
- Connects people with history.

Some people may resist the change, concerned about losing the legacy of the old name or identity. Even though we are in the business of preservation, it doesn't mean we can't change. Quite the opposite. We need to change if we want to continue to be relevant to the community and our audiences.

The National Trust for Historic Preservation published a statement that, although it was related to Confederate monuments, is equally relevant to history organizations that are evolving to better meet the communities' needs. The statement reads, "As preservationists, our goal is not to freeze places in time, and historic places should be allowed to evolve as their communities and individuals do. The purpose of preservation is not to stop change, but to offer tools that help a community manage change in thoughtful ways that do not disconnect the community from the full legacies of its past and the potential for its future."[19]

In response to that statement, the Ohio History Connection's Jamison Pack asks, "What is our role? If our role is to facilitate important conversations, and really understand the past, we must change. We must pay attention to where our communities are mentally, psychologically, intellectually. We must meet them there. Our challenge is to connect as many people as possible to history."

As you begin to think critically about your brand and whether your organization needs to rebrand, go beyond the name, fonts, and colors, and think about if and how your organization can better connect people with history through its programs, exhibits, collections, ambience, accessibility, and more. Are you doing it already? Does the public know? Will a rebrand help achieve that goal?

A good name and logo alone can't connect people to history or your organization. It can, however, improve name recognition and create a positive impression about your historic site or museum.

A good brand is like an open door. It invites people in and lets them know they are welcome.

NOTES

1. Casie Vance (executive director) in discussion with the author, May 2020.

2. Shoshana Wasserman (deputy director) in discussion with the author, July 2020.

3. Molly Alloy (co-director) in discussion with the author, May 2020.

4. Jorge Zamanillo (executive director) in discussion with the author, July 2020.

5. Forrest Rogers (interim executive director) in discussion with the author, July 2020.

6. Elizabeth P. Hynes (president, board of trustees) in discussion with the author, October 2020.

7. Angelica Diggs (former assistant director) in discussion with the author, September 2020.

8. Kathleen Powers (trustee) in discussion with the author, January 2021.

9. Jacob Thomas (executive director) in discussion with the author, May 2020.

10. Jamison Pack (chief marketing officer) in discussion with the author, May 2020.

11. Larissa Vigue Picard (executive director) in discussion with the author, May 2020.

12. Donna Odom (executive director) in discussion with the author, May 2020.

13. Diane A. Rhodes, "Perris Railway Museum Rolls into Future with New Name, Logo," *Press-Enterprise*, April 7, 2019, accessed August 10, 2020, https://www.pe.com/2019/04/07/perris-railway-museum-rolls-into-future-with-new-name-logo/.

14. Judy Zulfiqar (chief strategist, Watermark Associates) in discussion with the author, August 2020.

15. Pamela Junior (director, Two Mississippi Museums) in discussion with the author, August 2020.

16. Cindy Gardner (director, Mississippi Department of Archives and History, Museums Division) in discussion with the author, August 2020.

17. Katie Blount (director, Mississippi Department of Archives and History) in discussion with the author, August 2020.

18. Jamie Bosket (chief executive officer) in discussion with the author, June 2020.

19. "Confederate Monument—Frequently Asked Questions," National Trust for Historic Preservation, accessed December 28, 2020, https://savingplaces.org/confederate-monuments-faqs#.YDKOUGNOkzU.

Appendix

Short Summaries of the History Organizations

AMES HISTORY CENTER

Ames, Iowa
www.ameshistory.org

Mission

"Our mission is to engage our diverse public and provide unique opportunities to learn about Ames history."[1]

Interview(s)

Casie Vance, Executive Director

Former Name(s)

Ames Heritage Association
Ames Historical Society

Overview

Founded in 1980 as the Ames Heritage Association to save the community's first school from demolition, the Ames History Center is in a former office building in downtown Ames, home to Iowa State University. In 2005, the Ames Heritage Association became the Ames Historical Society. Three full-time staff members operate the museum and the original school, offering programs, rotating exhibits, and self-guided adult tours and field trips for about 7,000 people annually. The annual operating budget is approximately $180,000.

Reasons for Rebranding

- "Historical Society" did not appeal to families and young children.
- Old logo was difficult to work with and "looked historical."
- A capital campaign to upgrade the museum space was planned and they wanted the new branding in place when it kicked off.

Rebranding Costs: Less than $5,000

FIRST AMERICANS MUSEUM

Oklahoma City, Oklahoma
www.famok.org

Mission

"To serve as a dynamic center promoting awareness and educating the broader public about the unique cultures, diversity, history, contributions, and resilience of the First American Nations in Oklahoma today."[2]

Interview(s)

Shoshana Wasserman, Deputy Director

Former Name(s)

American Indians Cultural Center and Museum

Overview

The museum had not opened its doors when it rebranded as the First Americans Museum. The museum shares the collective histories of all thirty-nine tribal nations in Oklahoma, including their origin stories, material culture, and historical accounts from the First American's perspective. The 175,000-square-foot museum in Oklahoma City includes three galleries and the future FAMily Discovery Center. It also includes visitor amenities such as two theaters, a full-service restaurant, café, and museum store.

Reasons for Rebranding

- "American Indians" was inaccurate.
- "American Indians Cultural Center and Museum" was difficult to remember.
- Leadership wanted to revitalize the project prior to reopening with a more memorable, playful, and inclusive name.

Rebranding Costs: N/A

FIVE OAKS MUSEUM

Portland, Oregon
www.fiveoaksmuseum.org

Mission

"Five Oaks Museum's mission has not been revised to reflect the museum's new focus. Instead, the museum's guiding lights are its values of body, land, truth, justice, and community."[3]

Interview(s)

Molly Alloy, Co-Director

Former Name(s)

Washington County Museum

Overview

Located in the northwest part of the state, the museum had been struggling for several years. Under the leadership of co-directors Molly Alloy and Nathaniel Andreini, the team has transformed the museum into a vibrant cultural arts and history organization that tells stories through multiple perspectives. The museum has a staff of four employees, plus guest curators and volunteers, and an annual operating budget of approximately $400,000, half of which is subsidized by the county.

Reasons for Rebranding

- Wanted a less Eurocentric name that reflected the new, multilayered approach to storytelling.

- A new name would communicate to the public that the museum had changed.

Rebranding Costs: $30,000+

HISTORYMIAMI MUSEUM

Miami, Florida
www.HistoryMiami.org

Mission

"HistoryMiami Museum safeguards and shares Miami stories to foster learning, inspire a sense of place, and cultivate an engaged community. Through exhibitions, artistic endeavors, city tours, education, research, collections and publications, HistoryMiami Museum works to help everyone understand the importance of the past in shaping Miami's future."[4]

Interview(s)

Jorge Zamanillo, Executive Director
Michele Reese Granger, Marketing Director

Former Name(s)

Historical Museum of Southern Florida
HistoryMiami

Overview

Founded in 1940, HistoryMiami Museum consists of two adjacent buildings totaling approximately 75,000 square feet. The museum is dedicated to "telling Miami's stories" through exhibits, an ongoing oral history project, programs, tours, and events. It had undergone a major rebranding in 2010. The museum employs just under fifty people, about half of whom work part-time. It has an annual operating budget of approximately $6 million and a $17 million endowment. The museum receives county funding.

Reasons for Rebranding

- Formally add "Museum" to the HistoryMiami branding.
- Wanted a more versatile color palette that people would associate with Miami.
- ADA accessibility was key.

Rebranding Costs: N/A

MOAB MUSEUM

Moab, Utah
www.moabmuseum.org

Mission

"Our mission is to share stories. We seek to educate and inspire our community about the cultural and natural history of Moab and the Canyonlands region."[5]

Interview(s)

Forrest Rogers, Interim Executive Director

Former Name(s)

Moab Museum
Dan O'Laurie Canyon Country Museum
Dan O'Laurie Museum
Museum of Moab
Moab Museum of Natural and Cultural History (briefly)

Overview

After deciding against building a new, $60 million, state-of-the-art museum, the board decided to renovate the existing museum space, reinvent the exhibits, and change the focus from objects to stories. Two full-time employees and several part-time staff work at the museum, which welcomes about 7,000 visitors per year. The operating budget is $250,000, about 60 percent of which comes from the county.

Reasons for Rebranding

- Signal a change in the museum to the public.
- Simplicity.
- Return to its original name.

Rebranding Costs: $50,000–$75,000

MONTCLAIR HISTORY CENTER

Montclair, NJ
www.montclairhistory.org

Mission

"Our mission is to preserve, educate, and share. We preserve our local history through our historical buildings, artifacts and documents. We educate the community on local history and its importance through programs, advocacy and exhibits. We share the stories and history of the people who have shaped Montclair."[6]

Interview(s)

Elizabeth Hynes, President, Board of Trustees
Kathleen Powers, Member, Board of Trustees
Angelica Diggs, Former Assistant Director

Former Name(s):

Montclair Historical Society

Overview

The Montclair Historical Society underwent a transformation in 2014 to embrace the history of its flagship building, telling the story of when it was a YWCA for African American women and girls. That building, a 1796 home of one of Montclair's early entrepreneurs, is one of three eighteenth- and nineteenth-century buildings the Montclair History Center maintains on two acres of land about seventeen miles from New York City. The Montclair History Center employs two full-time and several part-time people with an annual operating budget of approximately $250,000. Approximately 7,000 people visit annually.

Reasons for Rebranding

- Reflect the fundamental changes that had occurred within the organization in recent years.
- Eliminate "historical society," which was a barrier to some audiences.
- More accurately describe it as a place to visit, rather than an organization to belong to.

Rebranding Costs: $8,000–$10,000

NORTHWEST MONTANA HISTORY MUSEUM

Kalispell, Montana
www.nwmthistory.org

Mission

"The Northwest Montana Historical Society is dedicated to the cultural and educational enrichment of the community through acquisition, preservation, and display of material related to local history, and to the involvement of the public of museum programs through research, community events, and volunteer opportunities."[7]

Interview(s)

Jacob Thomas, Executive Director

Former Name(s)

Northwest Montana Historical Society
Northwest Montana Heritage, Education, and Cultural Center
Central School Museum
Museum at Central School

Overview

Located in a public school built in 1894, the museum was created when local preservationists saved the building from demolition in the late 1990s. On the road to Glacier National Park, the museum shares local history and is actively used for museum events and as a rental space. There is one full-time employee and volunteers who "run the front of the house" on an operating budget of $144,000. About 15,000 people visit the museum, attend events, or rent events annually.

Reasons for Rebranding

- Confusion over the name "Museum at Central School."
- Tell the public that the museum is about the history of northwest Montana.

Rebranding Costs: Approximately $4,000

OHIO HISTORY CONNECTION

Columbus, Ohio
www.ohiohistory.org

Mission

"We spark discovery of Ohio's stories. Embrace the present, share the past and transform the future."[8]

Interview(s)

Jamison Pack, Chief Marketing Officer

Former Name(s)

Ohio Historical Society

Overview

Founded in 1885 as a collecting institution, today the Ohio History Connection is responsible for the state's historic preservation office, state archives, and local history office. It maintains a museum and a recreated nineteenth-century town. The Ohio History Connection also oversees a network of almost sixty museums, historic houses, archeological sites, boats, bridges, natural history sites, and canal locks located throughout the state. These sites are collectively visited by over 400,000 people annually. The operating budget is over $20 million, including allocations from the state.

Reasons for Rebranding

- "Historical society" was a barrier to certain demographics, particularly families.

- The name did not reflect the organization's wide reach or multifaceted responsibilities throughout the state.

Rebranding Costs: Over $350,000

PEJEPSCOT HISTORY CENTER

Brunswick, Maine
www.pejepscothistory.org

Mission

"Pejepscot History Center preserves, interprets, and promotes the rich history of Brunswick, Topsham, and Harpswell, Maine, through its collections, programs, and historic house museums."[9]

Interview(s)

Larissa Vigue Picard, Executive Director

Former Names(s)

Pejepscot Historical Society

Overview

Founded in 1889, the Pejepscot History Center serves three towns (Brunswick, Harpswell, and Topsham) on Maine's coast. Its three historic buildings include a museum and research center, the home of a Civil War hero, and a Victorian "time capsule" of three generations of the same family. The Pejepscot History Center is operated by two full-time employees and a part-time development manager. Its operating budget is $240,000.

Reasons for Rebranding

- "Historical Society" did not appeal to the museum's expanding audience of younger people.
- Logo was too site-specific.

Rebranding Costs: Less than $10,000

SOCIETY FOR HISTORY AND RACIAL EQUITY

Kalamazoo, Michigan
www.Sharekazoo.org

Mission

"The Society for History and Racial Equity has a dual mission of educating the community on the importance of our region's African American heritage and fostering connections and conversations on race and providing awareness of racism and the broad societal benefits of its elimination."[10]

Interview(s)

Donna Odom, Executive Director

Former Name(s)

Southwest Michigan Black History Society

Overview

Founded in 2003, the Society for History and Racial Equity began as a historical society dedicated to preserving and sharing Black history in southwest Michigan. Although SHARE has office space, they do not have a historical site to maintain. In 2010, the organization became involved in leading programs that promote racial equity and healing. The organization now has a dual mission of collecting Black history and promoting racial healing. There are three part-time staff members and an operating budget of $125,000.

Reasons for Rebranding

- Cumbersome name that no one could remember.
- Wanted a new name that reflected the dual mission.

Rebranding Costs: Less than $5,000

SOUTHERN CALIFORNIA RAILWAY MUSEUM

Perris, California
www.socalrailway.org

Mission

"To preserve and display artifacts and documents of the rail transportation industry in order to educate the public on the technology, history, and impact of the rail transportation industry in the west and more specifically in Southern California."[11]

Interview(s)

Judy Zulfiqar, Chief Strategist, Watermark Associates

Former Name(s)

Orange Empire Traction Company
Orange Empire Trolley Museum
Orange Empire Railway Museum

Overview

Founded in 1956 when freeways were replacing railways in Southern California, the organization is located on nearly 100 acres filled with decommissioned trolleys and trains that visitors can explore, ride on, and even be a conductor. The museum hosts several special events annually, such as a Day with Thomas and a Polar Express that draw thousands of visitors. The museum has a staff of five employees, over 1,500 volunteers, and an operating budget of over $1 million. Including the special events, the museum welcomes more than 100,000 visitors annually.

Reasons for Rebranding

- "Orange Empire Railway Museum" created confusion over where the museum is located.

Rebranding Costs: N/A

TWO MISSISSIPPI MUSEUMS

Jackson, Mississippi
www.mdah.ms.gov/2MM

Mission

"The Museum of Mississippi History encourages people to explore and appreciate our state's history. We present rich and complex stories that illustrate how our shared past influences our future together."[12]

"The Mississippi Civil Rights Museum shares the stories of a Mississippi movement that changed the nation. The museum promotes a greater understanding of the Mississippi Civil Rights Movement and its impact by highlighting the strength and sacrifices of its peoples."[13]

Interview(s)

Katie Blount, Director, Mississippi Department of Archives and History
Cindy Gardner, Museum Division Director
Pamela Junior, Director, Two Mississippi Museums

Former Name(s)

Old Capital Museum

Overview

When Hurricane Katrina blew the roof off the Old Capital Museum, a lengthy process started to create a new museum dedicated to Mississippi history. Simultaneously, an effort was underway to create a civil rights museum that concentrates on seminal years in the civil rights movement—1945 to 1975. The state ultimately decided to create the two museums side by side, separated by "an inch of caulk." The concept of "Two Mississippi Museums" was born. Today, the Two Mississippi Museums share an entrance, visitors' desk, gift shop, and staff of eleven. The state funds the museums through an annual appropriation of about $1.7 million. The Mississippi Department of Archives and History is expected to contribute $800,000 annually.

Reasons for Rebranding

- Desire to show that the two museums worked together to tell the complete history of Mississippi.

Rebranding Costs: N/A, rolled into museum opening

VIRGINIA MUSEUM OF HISTORY AND CULTURE

Richmond, Virginia
www.virginiahistory.org

Mission

"Connecting people to America's past through the unparalleled story of Virginia. By collecting, preserving, and interpreting the Commonwealth's history, we link past with present and inspire future generations."[14]

Interview(s)

Jamie Bosket, Chief Executive Officer

Former Name(s)

Virginia Historical and Philosophical Society
Virginia Historical Society

Overview

Founded in 1831, the organization includes a research library and a museum that tells a comprehensive history of Virginia. After several years of research, community involvement, and strategic planning, the museum has expanded its public programming and exhibitions to tell "a more inclusive story to a more inclusive audience." It has an operating budget of $8 to $8.5 million and an endowment of over $60 million and hosts approximately 110,000 visitors annually.

Reasons for Rebranding

- Wanted a new name that reflected the "reimagined" museum.
- Wanted a more inclusive-sounding name.
- "Historical Society" was a barrier to demographic audiences.

Rebranding Costs: Approximately $250,000 ($50,000 for research/design, $100,000 for implementation, $100,000 for increased marketing)

NOTES

1. "Home," Ames History Museum, accessed March 1, 2021, http://ameshistory .org/.

2. "About Us," First Americans Museum, accessed March 1, 2021, https://famok.org/about-us/.

3. "Our Values in Action," Five Oaks Museum, accessed March 1, 2021, https://fiveoaksmuseum.org/our-values-in-action-2020/.

4. "About the Museum," HistoryMiami Museum, accessed March 1, 2021, https://www.historymiami.org/museum/.

5. "About Moab Museum," Moab Museum, accessed March 1, 2021, https://moabmuseum.org/about/.

6. "Mission and History," Montclair History Center, accessed March 1, 2021, https://www.montclairhistory.org/new-mission-and-goals.

7. "About," Northwest Montana History Museum, accessed March 1, 2021, http://www.nwmthistory.org/about/.

8. "About Us," Ohio History Connection, accessed March 1, 2021, https://www.ohiohistory.org/about-us.

9. "About," Pejepscot History Center, accessed March 1, 2021, https://pejepscothistorical.org/about-us/mission.

10. "Home Page," Society for History and Racial Equity, accessed March 1, 2021, http://sharekazoo.org/.

11. "Southern California Railway Museum, Inc," Charity Navigator, accessed March 1, 2021, https://www.charitynavigator.org/ein/956102211.

12. "One Mississippi, Many Stories," Museum of Mississippi History, accessed March 1, 2021, https://mmh.mdah.ms.gov/story/one-mississippi-many-stories-0.

13. "About the Museum," Mississippi Museum of Civil Rights, accessed March 1, 2021, http://mcrm.mdah.ms.gov/story/about-the-museum.

14. "Our Vision, Values, and Mission," Virginia Museum of History and Culture, accessed March 1, 2021, https://www.virginiahistory.org/about-us/our-mission-vision-values.

Index

About the Author

Jane Mitchell Eliasof is the executive director of the Montclair History Center, an independent, not-for-profit organization dedicated to preserving local history, educating the community about it and its importance, and sharing the stories of the people who have shaped the community. During her tenure at the Montclair History Center, Jane led the rebranding from the Montclair Historical Society to appeal to a wider, younger, more diverse audience. She also directed the reinterpretation of a 1796 home to include its history as a segregated YWCA for African American women and girls, expanding the stories the Montclair History Center tells to reflect the rich diversity of and be relevant to the community. Jane has presented on a wide variety of topics and written numerous articles on local history and museums. She coauthored a chapter, "Race and Ethnicity in Historic House Museums," in *Reinventing the Historic House Museum*, edited by Kenneth Turino and Max van Balgooy (2019). Prior to her work in the history field, Jane spent more than twenty-five years designing and writing marketing, educational, and training programs for the health care industry. In 2010, she opted to use her expertise to further a cause she has always been passionate about—history and historic preservation.

Lightning Source UK Ltd.
Milton Keynes UK
UKHW021429210622
404747UK00003B/82